To Cheryl:
God's richest blessings
on you.

Debbie Busenkell

MANNA FROM HEAVEN

Delicious low-fat recipes inspired by great Bible stories

MANNA FROM HEAVEN

Delicious low-fat recipes inspired by great Bible stories

Debbie Busenkell

1stbooks – rev. 8/17/00

ABOUT THE BOOK

Manna From Heaven combines truths from classical Bible stories with delicious, healthy, low-fat recipes named for those stories. Many of the recipes have been developed over a period of twenty years. Following the chronological order of the Bible, foods from the fifty-two recipes (one for every week in the year) include such imaginative and delightful palate-pleasers as Garden of Eden Salad with Paradise Dressing, Spicy Lentil Soup similar to that for which Esau sold his birthright, King David's Beef Stew (fit for a king), Hearts of Palm Salad to celebrate Palm Sunday, a scrumptious Chocolate Cherry Torte to celebrate Jesus choosing His twelve apostles, and even a modern interpretation of manna itself.

Although inspired by ancient stories, these foods are up-to-the-minute in nutrition and health, and a tabulation of calories, fat, and sodium for each is included. Drawn from many countries, these foods help to illustrate the timeless teachings of God's Word.

ACKNOWLEDGMENTS

My heartfelt gratitude is extended to many people.

My **Heavenly Father**, who loves me and accepts me unconditionally. He is the One with whom I enjoy a nurturing, loving relationship. I am eternally grateful to Him for allowing His Son, Jesus Christ, to come to earth and shed His precious blood on the cross for all of my sins.

Jesus Christ, who was willing to die for all my sins. He's my Savior, my Lord, and my friend, my healer, and my deliverer.

The **Holy Spirit**, who is my teacher, my counselor, and my comforter. He guided me through this book.

My earthly **parents**, who set a strong example of commitment and perseverance. They encouraged me to pursue my interests in cooking and baking, and they ate my successes and failures.

My sister, **Jan**, who was the instrument who led me to Christ in 1973.

Dave Hocking, who gave me a strong foundation in the Word of God, under the inspiration of the Holy Spirit.

Bob Branch, Pastor of Springs Community Church, for reviewing this manuscript.

Kenneth Copeland Ministries, who were kind enough to allow me to use their ministries' "Prayer for Salvation and Baptism in the Holy Spirit." Reproduced with permission of Kenneth Copeland Ministries, Inc., Fort Worth, Texas 76192. *Our Covenant With God* by Kenneth Copeland, copyright 1980.

And to my dear husband, Rick, who has always encouraged me to write a cookbook and has tirelessly worked with me in the editing of this manuscript.

Thank you, one and all!

TABLE OF CONTENTS

FOREWORD

Welcome to a journey through Bible history, from Genesis to Revelation, as you enjoy some of my favorite recipes, which can be shared with your family and friends.

Throughout the pages of the Bible the message is the same, God loves us and created us to have a personal relationship with Him through His Son, Jesus Christ. In Deuteronomy 6, verse 5, the Scriptures tell us to "love the Lord your God with all your heart, all your soul, and all your strength." In verses 24 and 25, the "Lord our God has commanded us to obey all these laws and to fear him for our own prosperity and well being . . . For we are righteous when we obey all the commands the Lord our God has given us." We are deemed righteous by God when we trust Him. We are to teach these laws to our children when we are home and when we are away from home, when we are lying down to rest, and when we are getting up. The stories in this book are wonderful examples of ordinary people who trusted God and were used greatly by Him to help the people He loves. God invites us to live a life of great adventure in loving and serving Him.

In this book you will enjoy, perhaps for the first time, some of these great stories and their spiritual truths. I have used the New Living Translation of the Bible for the direct quotes, which makes this a book that is easy, fun, and enjoyable to read, whether it's as a devotion, as a bedtime story, or at any time. I've selected titles for the recipes which will bring remembrance to the story connected with that title. This can be used as a great conversation opener and teaching tool for people of all ages.

In this book I've tried to bring together two of my great loves -- the Bible and cooking. For me, spiritual manna is eating the Word daily by reading the Bible with an open heart and mind and applying it to my life with the help of the Holy Spirit, just as I eat physical manna every day to sustain my life.

I believe this spiritual manna, the great truths and principles of the Bible, needs to be read and recounted to ourselves and our children to learn what God has done and will continue to do in miraculous acts for those who put their trust in Him and obey Him. In the physical realm, God has given us teachers to help guide us to eat foods that are healthy for our bodies.

The recipes are healthful and low in fat. They can be prepared by adults and some can be prepared by children under the supervision of an adult. The amounts for calories, fat, and sodium for each recipe were obtained from a variety of sources. Some recipes contain white flour, white sugar, and "lite" butter. The preparation of these recipes are optional, based on one's dietary and personal preferences.

This cookbook evolved slowly. In January of 1997 I began to pray and ask God what He wanted me to do. Gradually the ideas came about for this book and the process of how to assemble it. This book is, and continues to be, a walk of faith, not of sight. It is my prayer that this cookbook will be an eternal blessing in your life.

Debbie Busenkell
Temecula, CA
October, 1999

THE GARDEN OF EDEN

In the beginning God created the heavens and the earth. The earth was empty, a formless mass cloaked in darkness. And the Spirit of God was hovering over its surface. Then God said, "Let there be light," and there was light. And God saw that it was good. Then he separated the light from the darkness. God called the light "day" and the darkness "night." Together these made up one day.

And God said, "Let there be space between the waters, to separate water from water." And so it was. God made this space to separate the waters above from the waters below. And God called the space "sky." This happened on the second day.

And God said, "Let the waters beneath the sky be gathered into one place so the dry ground may appear." And so it was. God named the dry ground "land" and the water "seas." And God saw that it was good. Then God said, "Let the land burst forth with every sort of grass and seed-bearing plant. And let there be trees that grow seed-bearing fruit. The seeds will then produce the kinds of plants and trees from which they came." And so it was. The land was filled with seed-bearing plants and trees, and their seeds produced plants and trees of like kind. And God saw that it was good. This all happened on the third day. *Gen. 1:1-13.*

On the fourth day the sun, moon, and stars were created. The birds and the fish came into being on the fifth day.

And God said, "Let the earth bring forth every kind of animal -- livestock, small animals, and wildlife." And so it was. God made all sorts of wild animals, livestock, and small animals, each able to reproduce more of its own kind. And God saw that it was good.

Then God said, "Let us make people in our image, to be like ourselves. They will be masters over all life -- the fish in the sea, the birds in the sky, and all the livestock, wild animals, and small animals."

So God created people in his own image. God patterned them after himself; male and female he created them.

God blessed them and told them, "Multiply and fill the earth and subdue it. Be masters over the fish and birds and all the animals." And God said, "Look! I have given you the seed-bearing plants throughout the earth and all the fruit trees for your food. And I have given all the grasses and other green plants to the animals and birds for their food." And so it was. Then God looked over all he had made, and he saw that it was excellent in every way. This all happened on the sixth day.

So the creations of the heavens and the earth and everything in them was completed. On the seventh day, having finished his task, God rested from all his work. And God blessed the seventh day and declared it holy, because it was the day when he rested from his work of creation.

This is the account of the creation of the heavens and the earth. *Gen. 1:24-2:4.*

The Lord God placed the man in the Garden of Eden to tend and care for it. *Gen. 2:15.*

And the Lord God said, "It is not good for the man to be alone. I will make a companion who will help him." *Gen. 2:18.* So the Lord God caused Adam to fall into a deep sleep. He took one of Adam's ribs and closed up the place from which he had taken it. Then the Lord God made a woman from the rib and brought her to Adam.

"At last!" Adam exclaimed. "She is part of my own flesh and bone. She will be called 'woman,' because she is taken out of man." *Gen. 2:21-23.*

Even though Adam was surrounded by plenty of food and animals and winged creatures of every kind, he was still *lonely.* God created a woman named Eve to *complete* him.

DID YOU KNOW?

Spiritual friendship is the kind of companionship God intends for His children to have. This is where two people nurture each other's spiritual lives. Its primary focus is on the deeper issues of life. We are made complete through the friendship of others as we travel along on our spiritual journey.

Garden of Eden Salad with Paradise Dressing

This delicious salad of fruits and vegetables will delight you today as it might have delighted Adam and Eve at the dawn of time.

Salad:

5 cups of <u>clean</u>, torn greens (romaine, red leaf, Boston bib, curly leaf, or any mix)
1-1/2 cups of fresh fruit, sliced and/or cut-up into bite-size pieces
1/4 cup nuts, chopped (walnuts, pecans, almonds)

(1) Wash and dry greens. Chill for about 1 hour.
(2) Chill plates for at least 30 minutes before serving salad. Chop or slice fruits in complementary shapes. Chop nuts. Place greens equally on salad plates, then fruits, nuts, and dressing.
(3) Serve at once.

Paradise Dressing:

      1/2 cup fat-free plain yogurt
      2 tablespoons honey
      5 teaspoons fresh lime, lemon, or orange juice*
      1 tablespoon powdered sugar
      1/2 teaspoon shredded lime, lemon, or orange peel

(1) Place all ingredients except <u>peel</u> in a blender and whip for 30 seconds. Add peel. Chill for 1 hour.

     * Use the same flavor juice as the peel.

Salad:
Servings: 4
Calories: 69
Fat (g.): 0
Sodium: 5 mg.

Dressing:
Servings: 4
Calories: 23
Fat (g.): 0
Sodium: 0 mg.

NOAH AND THE GREAT FLOOD

As the years went by most people chose to do evil instead of obeying God. However, there was one man who believed in God and obeyed Him. Noah was that man. He walked with God and taught the principles of obedience, faithfulness, and patience to his sons and their wives.

God loved Noah and told him about a flood He was going to send upon the earth. Noah was told by God to build an ark, which is a large boat. **So Noah did everything exactly as God had commanded him.** *Gen. 6:22.* It took Noah over 100 years to build the ark! When judgment came on the people of the earth by way of the flood, Noah, his wife, his sons, and their wives were spared. God is faithful to those who trust and obey Him.

DID YOU KNOW?

In "walking with God," Noah displayed a spirit, an attitude, and a character that made him accepted and approved for the most intimate spiritual relationship. He manifested qualities of soul that endeared him to the Lord.

Watermelon Ark with Fruit Salad and Dressing

When this beautiful fruit salad is presented within this miniature ark, it will bring joy to your family of hungry travelers, even though it won't last for forty days and forty nights. It's especially effective for a summer children's party when, used as a centerpiece, it has plastic animals and people in and around the ark.

1 long watermelon
Strawberries, peaches, red and/or green seedless grapes, melons (cantaloupe, honeydew, casaba, etc.), pineapple

(1) Cut watermelon in half horizontally.
(2) Scoop out watermelon flesh with a "melon baller" or cut in small chunks and lift out with a utensil.
(3) Cut other fruit into a variety of bite-size pieces (wedges, balls, cubes). Place in ark.
(4) Serve with lemon dressing over fruit or on the side for dipping.

<u>Lemon Dressing</u>:

    8-ounce container, low-fat lemon yogurt
    1 teaspoon lemon rind, grated

(1) Stir yogurt and serve with fruit.

Salad:
Servings: 10
Calories: 100/cup
Fat (g): 0
Sodium: 10 mg.

Dressing:
Servings: 6
Calories: 8/tablespoon
Fat (g.): 0
Sodium: 8 mg.

ABRAM GETS A NEW NAME

Abram and his wife Sarai were imperfect-but-willing instruments God used to accomplish His perfect plan. God asked these two people to leave the comfort and familiarity of a pagan world to follow Him. **Then the Lord told Abram, "Leave your country, your relatives, and your father's house, and go to the land that I will show you. I will cause you to become the father of a great nation. I will bless you and make you famous, and I will make you a blessing to others. I will bless those who bless you and curse those who curse you. All the families of the earth will be blessed through you."** *Gen. 12:1-3.*

So Abram departed as the Lord has instructed him . . . Abram was 75 years old when he left Haran. . . *Gen. 12:4.*

Then the Lord appeared to Abram and said, "I am going to give this land to your offspring." And Abram built an altar to God there. *Gen. 12:7.* This was just one of many altars Abram was to build. God promised that through this one man, Abram, the land and all his descendants would be blessed. This is called *covenant relationship.* Abram and Sarai wanted a child very much even though they were advanced in age. God had said they would have one. **And Abram believed the Lord and the Lord declared him righteous because of his faith.** *Gen. 15:6.*

During their pilgrimage the pair strayed from God's will many times. They gave into fear and dishonest dealings with Pharaoh and Abimelech. They struggled to persevere and tried to raise up a line of descendants through Sarai's servant, Hagar. Strife and jealousy erupted which led to irresponsible behavior by both. Abram and Sarai's mutual affection and respect survived through stresses and fleshly temptation. *Yet, these failures never lessened God's love for them nor altered His commitment to His promises.*

After Abram returned from his victory over Kedorlaomer and his allies, he cried out to God. **"O Sovereign Lord, what good are all your blessings when I don't even have a son?"** *Gen. 15:2.* **Then the Lord brought Abram outside beneath the night sky and told him, "Look up to the heavens and count the stars if you can. Your descendants will be like that -- too many to count." And Abram believed the Lord, and the Lord declared him righteous because of his faith.** *Gen. 15:5-6.*

When Abram was ninety-nine years old, the Lord appeared to him and said, "I am the Lord God Almighty; serve me faithfully and live a blameless life. I will make a covenant with you by which I will guarantee to make you into a mighty nation." At this, Abram fell face down in the dust. Then God said to him, "This is my covenant with you: I will make you the father of not just one nation, but a multitude of nations. What's more, I am changing you name. It will no longer be Abram; now you will be known as Abraham, for

you will be the father of many nations. I will give you millions of descendants who will represent many nations. Kings will be among them!”

“I will continue this everlasting covenant between us, generation after generation. It will continue between me and your offspring forever. I will always be your God and the God of your descendants after you. Yes, I will give all this land to you and your offspring forever. And I will be their God.” *Gen. 17:1-8.*

DID YOU KNOW?

The Abrahamic Covenant contains the following elements: (1) “I (God) will make of thee a great nation,” (2) “I (God) will bless thee (temporarily and spiritually),” (3) “I (God) will make thy name great,” (4) and “Thou shalt be a blessing.”

Jews and born-again Christians have this covenant relationship with God through Abraham, with all the same rights and privileges.

Flapjacks to Pancakes a la Bananas

Sliced bananas make a healthful topping for pancakes, once commonly called flapjacks. You might want to change *your* name for a stack of these mouth-watering gems.

Non-stick vegetable oil cooking spray
1 cup pancake mix
1 egg
2/3 cup non-fat milk, scant
1/3 cup applesauce
1 teaspoon vanilla
3 bananas, sliced or large diced*
“Lite” maple syrup

(1) Heat griddle or large frying pan over medium-high heat. Sprinkle with a few drops of water. When droplets “dance,” spray with cooking spray.
(2) While pan is heating up, mix all ingredients together until just blended (except bananas and maple syrup).
(3) Cut up fruit and warm syrup.
(4) Scoop pancake batter up in 1/4 cup measuring cup and dump onto prepared pan. When bubbles “pop,” turn with pancake turner. Cook on other side 1-2 minutes or until golden brown.
(5) Place pancakes on plate. Place bananas and syrup over pancakes.

* May substitute any number of fruits alone or in any combination: strawberries, blackberries, boysenberries, raspberries, peaches, plums, nectarines, etc.

Servings: 3
Calories: 400
Fat (g): 3
Sodium: 400 mg.

GOD KEEPS HIS PROMISE

Then God added, "Regarding Sarai, your wife -- her name will no longer be Sarai; from now on you will call her Sarah. And I will bless her and give you a son from her. Yes, I will bless her richly, and she will become the mother of many nations. Kings will be among her descendants!"

Then Abraham bowed down to the ground, but he laughed to himself in disbelief. "How could I become a father at the age of one hundred?" he wondered. "Besides, Sarah is ninety; how could she have a baby?" *Gen. 17:15-17.*

But God replied, "Sarah, your wife, will bear you a son. You will name him Isaac, and I will confirm my everlasting covenant with him and his descendants. But my covenant is with Isaac, who will be born to you and Sarah about this time next year." *Gen. 17:19.*

Then the Lord said to Abraham, "Why did Sarah laugh (when she heard her husband and some men talk about the baby)? Why did she say, 'Can an old woman like me have a baby?' Is anything too hard for the Lord?" *Gen. 18:13-14a.*

Then the Lord did exactly what he had promised. Sarah became pregnant, and she gave a son to Abraham in his old age. It all happened at the time God had said it would. *Gen. 21:1,2.*

DID YOU KNOW?

The divine name *El Shadday* sends a message that "Nothing is impossible with God who is all-powerful and all-sufficient."

God Promises a Miracle Meatloaf

Just as Abraham and Sarah waited a long time for a son, you've waited a long time without tasting a meatloaf as good as this one. It's a miracle!

Non-stick vegetable oil cooking spray
14 ounces ground turkey (10% or less fat)
2 eggs, lightly beaten
18 saltine crackers, crumbled
1/4 cup uncooked oatmeal
3 tablespoons oat bran
1 cup frozen green peas
1 cup onion, finely chopped

1/2 cup frozen corn
1/4 cup parsley, chopped*
1 tablespoon Worcestershire sauce
1 clove garlic, minced
1/4 teaspoon salt
1/2 teaspoon freshly ground pepper
3/4 cup tomato sauce

(1) Preheat oven to 400 degrees.
(2) In large bowl, thoroughly mix all ingredients. (Hands work best).
(3) Turn into a sprayed 9" x 5" loaf pan.
(4) Bake 60-70 minutes. Let stand 15 minutes before turning out on a serving plate.

* Cilantro, instead of parsley, gives meatloaf a great zip!

Servings: 8
Calories: 160
Fat (g.): 7
Sodium: 160 mg.

ESAU SELLS HIS BIRTHRIGHT

As the boys (Esau and Jacob, the sons of Isaac by Rebekah) **grew up, Esau became a skillful hunter, a man of the open fields, while Jacob was the kind of person who liked to stay at home. Isaac loved Esau in particular because of the wild game he brought home, but Rebekah favored Jacob.**

One day when Jacob was cooking some stew, Esau arrived home exhausted and hungry from a hunt. Esau said to Jacob, "I'm starved! Give me some of that red stew you've made."

Jacob replied, "All right, but trade me your birthright for it."

"Look, I'm dying of starvation!" said Esau. "What good is my birthright to me now?"

So Jacob insisted, "Well then, swear to me right now that it is mine." So Esau swore an oath, thereby selling all his rights as the firstborn to his younger brother. Then Jacob gave Esau some bread and lentil stew. Esau ate and drank and went on about his business, indifferent to the fact that he had given up his birthright. *Gen. 25:27-34*

When Isaac was old and almost blind, he called to Esau, his older son, and said, "My son?"

"Yes, Father?" Esau replied.

"I am an old man now," Isaac said, "and I expect every day to be my last. Take your bow and quiver full of arrows out into the open country, and hunt some wild game for me. Prepare it just the way I like it so it's savory and good, and bring it here for me to eat. Then I will pronounce the blessing that belongs to you, my firstborn son, before I die."

But Rebekah overheard the conversation. So when Esau left to hunt for the wild game, she said to her son Jacob, "I overheard your father asking Esau to prepare him a delicious meal of wild game. He wants to bless Esau in the Lord's presence before he dies. Now, my son, do exactly as I tell you. Go out to the flocks and bring me two fine young goats. I'll prepare your father's favorite dish from them. Take the food to your father; then he can eat it and bless you instead of Esau before he dies." *Gen. 27:1-10.*

So Jacob followed his mother's instructions . . . *Gen. 27:14a.* He brought her two freshly killed goats and put on special clothing his mother had made so he would feel hairy like his brother Esau. When the food and clothing were ready, Jacob went to where his father was.

So Jacob went over and kissed him. And when Isaac caught the smell of his clothes, he was finally convinced, and he blessed his son. He said, "The smell of my son is the good smell of the open fields that the Lord has blessed. May God always give you plenty of dew for healthy crops and good harvests of grain and wine. May you be the master of your brothers. May all your mother's sons bow low before you. All who curse you are cursed, and all who bless you are blessed." *Gen. 27:27-29.*

When Esau returned from the fields and found out that Jacob had stolen his first-born blessing, he let out a bitter cry. Esau said bitterly, "No wonder his name is Jacob, for he has deceived me twice, first taking my birthright and now stealing my blessing." *Gen. 27:36.*

Esau pleaded, "Not one blessing left for me? O my father, bless me, too!" Then Esau broke down and wept.

His father, Isaac, said to him, "You will live off the land and what it yields, and you will live by your sword. You will serve your brother for a time, but then you will shake loose from him and be free." *Gen. 27:38-40.*

The fruit of that deception and those lies destroyed the family life of Rebekah, Jacob, and Esau. Even so, God's plan for His kingdom was not thwarted by man's opposition, failure, or lack of faith. He is able to make His will prevail no matter what.

DID YOU KNOW?
Rebekah and Jacob knew that Jacob was the heir to God's promises through Abraham (Gen. 25:23 - 29:33), but they tried to use deceit to make God's plan happen their way. Of course, that never works and always causes pain somewhere else. God's in charge of the timetable of each of our lives. It's wise to move with the truth at His pace.

Spicy Lentil Soup

You don't have to sell *your* birthright to experience this traditional dish of the Middle East. Just enjoy it!

Non-stick olive oil cooking spray
2 cups dry lentils, rinsed
4-1/2 cups vegetable stock or bouillon cube reconstituted
1 14-1/2 oz. can of beef broth
1 large onion, chopped
2 celery stalks and tops, chopped
2 carrots, diced
1/2 cup green pepper, chopped
2 garlic cloves, minced
2 cups pureed tomatoes
1/4 cup lemon juice

2 tablespoon fresh parsley, chopped
1/2 teaspoon thyme
1/2 teaspoon tarragon
2 tablespoons "lite" soy sauce
2/3 cup Swiss cheese, shredded

(1) Place lentils in a Dutch oven covered with water. Add stock and simmer in the covered pot until tender, about 45 minutes.
(2) While the lentils are cooking, spray a large frying pan with cooking spray and sauté the onion, celery, carrots, green pepper, and garlic. Sauté for 3-5 minutes.
(3) Add this mixture to the cooked lentils. Add stock. Also add the tomatoes, lemon juice, parsley, seasoning, and soy sauce. Simmer for about 20-30 minutes or until soup is well-blended.
(4) When ready to serve, sprinkle cheese in bottom of the soup bowl and ladle in the soup.

Servings: 8
Calories: 286
Fat (g): 2.5
Sodium: 845 mg.

JACOB'S LADDER TO HEAVEN

Jacob left Beersheba and traveled toward Haran. At sundown he arrived at a good place to set up camp and stopped there for the night. Jacob found a stone for a pillow and lay down to sleep. As he slept, he dreamed of a stairway that reached from earth to heaven. And he saw the angels of God going up and down on it.

At the top of the stairway stood the Lord and he said, "I am the Lord, the God of your grandfather Abraham and the God of your father, Isaac. The ground you are lying on belongs to you. I will give it to you and your descendants. Your descendants will be as numerous as the dust of the earth. They will cover the land from east to west and from north to south. All the families of the earth will be blessed through you and your descendants. What's more, I will be with you, and I will protect you wherever you go. I will someday bring you safely back to this land. I will be with you constantly until I have finished giving you everything I have promised."

Then Jacob woke up and said, "Surely the Lord is in this place, and I wasn't even aware of it." He was afraid and said, "What an awesome place this is! It is none other than the house of God -- the gateway to heaven!" The next morning he got up very early. He took the stone he had used as a pillow and set it upright as a memorial pillar. Then he poured olive oil over it. He named the place Bethel -- "house of God" -- though the name of nearby village was Luz. *Gen. 28:10-19.*

DID YOU KNOW?
The true staircase between heaven and earth is the Son of Man, Jesus Christ. It is He who really bridges the interval between heaven and earth, God and man.

Jacob's Ladder Scalloped Potatoes

The potato slices in this dish look like stepping stones and will carry you and your tastebuds to heaven. Jacob would have wished he could have been with you to enjoy this dish!

Non-stick vegetable oil cooking spray
4 large Russet potatoes, peeled and thinly sliced
2 onions, finely chopped
1 packet Butter Buds
Freshly ground pepper to taste
2 cups 1% milk, hot
1-1/2 cups fat-free cheddar chees
Salt or Mrs. Dash to taste

(1) Preheat oven to 400 degrees.
(2) Spray a 9" x 13" glass baking dish with cooking spray. Place 2 sliced potatoes on bottom of pan in an overlap formation. Sprinkle all of onions on next. Sprinkle on Butter Buds. Repeat layer.
(3) Pour hot milk over potato/onion mixture. Sprinkle with cheddar cheese. Cover with aluminum foil and bake 1 hour. Remove foil and bake 15-20 minutes longer.

Servings: 8
Calories: 98:
Fat (g): 0.6
Sodium: 220 mg.

A PILE OF STONES

Then Jacob made this vow: "If God will be with me and protect me on this journey and give me food and clothing, and if he will bring me back safely to my father, then I will make the Lord my God. This memorial pillar will become a place for worshipping God, and I will give God a tenth of everything he gives me." *Gen. 28:20-22.*

The vow that Jacob made to God may not have been entirely honest, yet God still honored it and blessed him. He is willing to work with us even when we are selfish people. How gracious God is to those He loves!

DID YOU KNOW?
Jacob eventually matured to where he could be honest and humbly seek forgiveness.

A Pile of Stones Bubble Loaf

This loaf of bread looks like a pile of stones, but these rolls are light and fluffy. They would make a memorable addition to your next party.

Non-stick butter oil cooking spray
1 pkg. of frozen white dinner rolls
1/3 cup "lite" butter
3/4 cup sugar
2 teaspoons cinnamon

(1) Melt butter or margarine and place in a small bowl.
(2) Place sugar and cinnamon in another small bowl and mix well.
(3) Spray baking pan (I suggest an oval ceramic pan).
(4) Dip each frozen piece of dough first in butter, then roll around in sugar/cinnamon mixture. Place in pan about 1" apart.
(5) Let rise to quadruple in bulk in a warm place.
(6) Bake at 375 degrees for 30-35 minutes.

Servings: 18
Calories: 170
Fat (g): 4.6
Sodium: 366 mg.

Joseph's Coat of Many Colors

So Jacob settled again in the land of Canaan, where his father had lived.

This is the history of Jacob's family. When Joseph was seventeen years old, he often tended his father's flocks with his half brothers, the sons of his father's wives Bilhah and Zilpah. But Joseph reported to his father some of the bad things his brothers were doing. Now Jacob loved Joseph more than any of his children because Joseph had been born to him in his old age. So one day he gave Joseph a special gift -- a beautiful robe. But his brothers hated Joseph because of their father's partiality. They couldn't say a kind word to him.

One night Joseph had a dream and promptly reported the details to his brothers, causing them to hate him even more. "Listen to this dream," he announced. "We were out in the field tying up bundles of grain. My bundle stood up, and then your bundles all gathered around and bowed low before it!"

"So you are going to be king, are you?" his brothers taunted. And they hated him all the more for his dream and what he had said.

Then Joseph had another dream and told his brothers about it. "Listen to this dream," he said. **"The sun, moon, and eleven stars bowed down low before me!"** *Gen. 37:1-10.*

Loving deeply without limits and the hunger of not feeling deeply loved certainly caused relational difficulties in this family. Joseph was sold into Egyptian slavery by his brothers. Yet God worked His plan out in spite of man's desire to inflict pain onto another.

DID YOU KNOW?
Joseph was a very confident man who, through years of difficulties and suffering, developed mature self-assurance. Joseph was able to couple his knowledge of God with his self-assurance to ask God the question, "Lord, what do you want me to do?" He was free of the self-pitying attitude of, "Why me, Lord?" He also was a man of high personal integrity based on his relationship with God and allowing "himself to die that he might live."

Colorful Cobb Salad with Blue Cheese Dressing

Just as Joseph's coat had many rows of colors, this salad has many colorful rows of ingredients. You may toss the salad in the usual manner, or serve it with the ingredients still in rows. Either way, it's a delight to the eye just as Joseph's coat was.

5 cups fresh spinach, thoroughly washed and torn into bite-size pieces
3 hard-boiled eggs, finely chopped
1 cup tomatoes, finely chopped
1/3 cup scallions, finely chopped
6 slices crisp turkey bacon, crumbled
1/3 cup blue cheese

(1) In a low serving bowl, place spinach.
(2) Place alternative rows of egg, bacon, blue cheese, tomatoes, and scallions.
(3) Place dressing on salad -- toss (if desired).
(4) Place portions on chilled salad plates.

Blue Cheese Dressing:

3 ounces blue cheese
6 tablespoons fat-free plain yogurt
1/2 cup fat-free ricotta cheese
2 teaspoons white vinegar
1/8 teaspoon fresh-ground black pepper
1/2 teaspoon sugar

(1) Working in a small bowl, use fork to crumble blue cheese.
(2) Stir in 2 tablespoons of yogurt until smooth and creamy. Add ricotta cheese, vinegar, pepper, and remaining 4 tablespoons of yogurt.
(3) Using hand beater or electric mixer, beat together until well combined. Refrigerate to store. Stir before serving.

Salad:
Servings: 4
Calories: 234
Fat (g.): 1.5
Sodium: 582 mg.

Dressing:
Servings: 4
Calories: 78
Fat (g.): 1
Sodium: 120 mg.

VOICE IN THE BURNING BUSH

One day Moses was tending the flock of his father-in-law, Jethro, the priest of Midian, and he went deep into the wilderness near Sinai, the mountain of God. Suddenly, the angel of the Lord appeared to him as a blazing fire in a bush. Moses was amazed because the bush was engulfed in flames, but it didn't burn up. "Amazing!" Moses said to himself. "Why isn't that bush burning up? I must go over to see this."

When the Lord saw that he had caught Moses' attention, God called to him from the bush, "Moses! Moses!"

"Here I am!" Moses replied.

"Do not come any closer," God told him. "Take off your sandals, for you are standing on holy ground." Then he said, "I am the God of your ancestors - - the God of Abraham, the God of Isaac, and the God of Jacob." When Moses heard this, he hid his face in his hands because he was afraid to look at God.

Then the Lord told him, "You can be sure I have seen the misery of my people in Egypt. I have heard their cries for deliverance from their harsh slave drivers. Yes, I am aware of their suffering. So I have come to rescue them from the Egyptians and lead them out of Egypt into their own good and spacious land. It is a land flowing with milk and honey -- the land where the Canaanites, Hittites, Amorites, Perizzites, Hivites, and Jebusites live. The cries of the people of Israel have reached me, and I have seen how the Egyptians have oppressed them with heavy tasks. Now go, for I am sending you to Pharaoh. You will lead my people, the Israelites, out of Egypt."

"But who am I to appear before Pharaoh?" Moses asked God. "How can you expect me to lead the Israelites out of Egypt?"

Then God told him, "I will be with you. And this will serve as proof that I have sent you. When you have brought the Israelites out of Egypt, you will return here to worship God at this very mountain." *Ex. 3:1-12.*

After leaving Egypt and fleeing into the desert for protection, Moses found the solitude and time for quiet reflection his soul desperately needed. He gave time to growing in his relationship with God away from the responsibilities and distractions of Egypt. In the quietness of God's presence, he was able to look at himself and others honestly -- strengths and weaknesses. When God called him to ministry, he was able to admit his "weakness" and accept help -- God's help and man's help.

DID YOU KNOW?
The two-fold revelation was made to Moses by God in the burning bush:
(1) God had an eternal existence, and (2) God had a mission to deliver his own people.

Spicy Oven-Baked French Fries

Although not burning hot, these spicy baked potatoes are a tasty and healthful alternative to the usual deep-fat-fried french fries. God shouldn't have to speak to us from the burning bush to warn us about the dangers of fried foods.

Non-stick vegetable oil cooking spray
3 large Russet potatoes, scrubbed and cut into 1/4-inch "sticks"*
2 teaspoons oil
6 tablespoons Dijon mustard
   Paprika

(1) Preheat oven to 400 degrees. Spray a baking sheet.
(2) Whisk together oil and mustard in large mixing bowl. Add potatoes and toss to coat well.
(3) Using a slotted spoon, remove potatoes and spread on baking sheet. Sprinkle with paprika. Bake 30 minutes, turn fries over, and bake an additional 30 minutes. Potatoes are done when golden brown and crispy.

   *You may peel the potatoes, if desired.

Servings: 4
Calories: 88
Fat (g.): 2.3
Sodium: 470 mg.

Following a Cloud

When Pharaoh finally let the people go, God did not lead them on the road that runs through Philistine territory, even though that was the shortest way from Egypt to the Promised Land. God said, "If the people are faced with a battle, they might change their minds and return to Egypt." So God led them along a route through the wilderness toward the Red Sea, and the Israelites left Egypt like a marching army. *Ex. 13:17-18.*

Leaving Succoth, they camped at Etham on the edge of the wilderness. The Lord guided them by a pillar of cloud during the day and pillar of fire at night. That way they could travel whether it was day or night. And the Lord did not remove the pillar of cloud or pillar of fire from their sight. *Ex. 13:20-22.*

Then the angel of God, who had been leading the people of Israel, moved to a position behind them, and the pillar of cloud also moved around behind them. The cloud settled between the Israelite and Egyptian camps. As night came, the pillar of cloud turned into a pillar of fire, lighting the Israelite camp. But the cloud became darkness to the Egyptians, and they couldn't find the Israelites. *Ex. 14:19-20.*

The shortest path in life is not always the best. God often guides us through the scenic route of hills and valleys to test our faith and our commitment to Him by surrendering control of our lives to Him. This shows us again and again who He is and who we are.

DID YOU KNOW?
The pillar was a real sign of the real presence of Jehovah with his people.

Baked Meringue Clouds with Raspberries

These meringues, which look like little clouds, will lead you on to the Promised Land overflowing, not with "milk and honey," but with raspberries. They make a light and elegant dessert for special occasions.

Non-stick vegetable oil cooking spray
4 large egg whites, at room temperature
1/8 teaspoon cream of tartar
1 cup sugar

Meringues:

(1) Preheat oven to 200 degrees.

(2) Spray cooking oil on cookie sheets or line sheets with parchment paper.
(3) Beat egg whites with cream of tartar until stiff peaks form. Add half the sugar, 1 tablespoon at a time, continuing to beat until the meringue is very stiff and shiny. Fold in the remaining sugar.
(4) Spoon or pipe the meringue cookie mixture into tiny rounds on sheet. Bake until meringues are dry throughout, but not brown (about 1-1/2 to 2-1/2 hours). Test for doneness. If meringue crumbles with no sogginess, they're done. If baking on a "dry" (not humid) day, the meringues will probably be done in 1-1/2 hours.
(5) When meringues are completely dry, store covered in an airtight container, or freeze and serve straight from the freezer.

Topping:

1 10-ounce pkg. frozen raspberries,
Thawed fresh raspberries
Fresh mint

(1) Pour thawed berries from package and juice into a sieve that has a bowl below it. Press with the back of a large spoon to push all berry pulp into bowl.

Presentation:

(1) Gently spoon 2-3 tablespoons of berry puree onto salad-size serving plate. Swirl puree around plate in a creative way.
(2) Place a meringue in an off-center position. Spoon 2 more spoonfuls of puree over meringue. Place about 8 fresh raspberries randomly over the dessert and plate. Top with a sprig of mint.

Meringues:
Servings: 10
Calories: 60
Fat (g.): 0
Sodium: 25 mg.

Topping:
Servings: 6
Calories: 40
Fat (g.): 0
Sodium: 0

A PATH THROUGH THE RED SEA

Then Moses raised his hand over the sea, and the Lord opened up a path through the water with a strong east wind. The wind blew all that night, turning the seabed into dry land. So the people of Israel walked through the sea on dry ground, with walls of water on each side. Then the Egyptians -- all of Pharaoh's horses, chariots, and charioteers -- followed them across the bottom of the sea. But early in the morning, the Lord looked down on the Egyptian army from the pillar of fire and cloud, and threw them into confusion. Their chariot wheels began to come off, making their chariots impossible to drive. "Let's get out of here!" the Egyptians shouted. "The Lord is fighting for Israel against us!"

When all the Israelites were on the outside, the Lord said to Moses, "Raise your hand over the sea again. Then the waters will rush back over the Egyptian chariots and charioteers." So as the sun began to rise, Moses raised his hand over the sea. The water roared back into its usual place, and the Lord swept the terrified Egyptians into the surging currents. The waters covered all the chariots and charioteers -- the entire army of Pharaoh. Of all the Egyptians who had chased the Israelites into the sea, not a single one survived.

The people of Israel had walked through the middle of the sea on dry land, as the water stood up like a wall on both sides. This was how the Lord rescued Israel from the Egyptians that day. And the Israelites could see the bodies of the Egyptians washed up on the shore. When the people of Israel saw the mighty power that the Lord had displayed against the Egyptians, they feared the Lord and put their faith in him and in his servant Moses. *Ex. 14:21-31.*

Humanly speaking, with the sea before them, the Israelites faced certain destruction and seemingly would have cried out, "Let us alone." We would rather stay in sinful bondage than, with the courage of faith, make the effort to follow into "newness of life." Yet God knew his people and guided them one step at a time to victory. They made a choice to respond in faith -- walk between the massive walls of water that could easily have drowned them. Steps of faith require commitment to God, which results in growth in faith. Faith requires that we step out to receive all the blessings God has for us.

DID YOU KNOW?

God showed His omnipotence not only as a merciful deliverer but as the holy judge of the ungodly. God wanted his people to grow in fear (reverence) and in continued faith in Him as they had already shown.

A Path Through the Red Sea Crab Rolls

The split frankfurter roll symbolizes the parting of the Red Sea, and the crab mixture provides a maritime flavor. You don't have to wait for Moses to wave his hand in order to close up this sandwich and eat it.

1/2 cup fat-free mayonnaise
2 teaspoons fresh lemon juice
1-1/2 teaspoons Dijon-style mustard
1 teaspoon olive oil
3/4 teaspoon fresh tarragon, chopped*
1/4 teaspoon hot-pepper sauce
1/4 teaspoon salt
1/8 teaspoon black pepper
3/4 lb. imitation crab, diced
4 soft frankfurter rolls

(1) Whisk mayonnaise, lemon juice, mustard, oil, tarragon, pepper sauce, salt and pepper in medium-size bowl. Mix in crab; cover with plastic wrap, refrigerate for at least 1 hour.
(2) Gently open each roll; lightly toast. Fill with crab mixture.

*or 1/4 teaspoon dried tarragon

Servings: 4
Calories: 299
Fat (g.): 3
Sodium: 740 mg.

MANNA FROM HEAVEN

Then they (the Israelites) **left Elim and journeyed into the Sin Desert, between Elim and Mount Sinai. They arrived there a month after leaving Egypt. There, too, the whole community of Israel spoke bitterly against Moses and Aaron.**

"Oh, that we were back in Egypt," they moaned. "It would have been better if the Lord had killed us there! At least there we had plenty to eat. But now you have brought us into this desert to starve us to death."

Then the Lord said to Moses, "Look, I'm going to rain down food from heaven for you. The people can go out each day and pick up as much food as they need for that day. I will test them in this to see whether they will follow my instructions. Tell them to pick up twice as much as usual on the sixth day of each week." *Ex. 16:1-5.*

And the Lord said to Moses, "I have heard the people's complaints. Now tell them, 'In the evening you will have meat to eat, and in the morning you will be filled with bread. Then you will know that I am the Lord your God.' "

That evening vast numbers of quail arrived and covered the camp. The next morning the desert all around the camp was wet with dew. When the dew disappeared later in the morning, thin flakes, white like frost, covered the ground. The Israelites were puzzled when they saw it. "What is it?" they asked.

And Moses told them, "It is the food the Lord has given you. The Lord says that each household should gather as much as it needs. Pick up two quarts for each person."

So the people of Israel went out and gathered this food - some getting more, and some getting less. By gathering two quarts for each person, everyone had just enough. Those who gathered a lot had nothing left over, and those who gathered only a little had enough. Each family had just what it needed. *Ex. 16:11-18.*

In time, the food became known as manna. It was white like coriander seed, and it tasted like honey cakes. *Ex. 16:31.*

Then Moses gave them this command from the Lord: "Take two quarts of manna and keep it forever as a treasured memorial of the Lord's provision. By doing this, later generations will be able to see the bread that the Lord provided in the wilderness when he brought you out of Egypt."

Moses said to Aaron, "Get a container and put two quarts of manna into it. Then store it in a sacred place as a reminder for all future generations." Aaron did this, just as the

Lord had commanded Moses. He eventually placed it for safekeeping in the Ark of the Covenant. So the people of Israel ate manna for forty years until they arrived in the land of Canaan, where there were crops to eat. *Ex. 16:32-35.*

DID YOU KNOW?

The translation of the word *manna* is "What is it?" When the Israelites saw it lying on the ground they said to one another, "What is it?" For they knew not what it was. If the children of Israel tried to the save the manna over night, except on the sixth day, they would find that it was full of maggots and smelled terrible.

Manna From Heaven Muffins

Manna tasted sweet, and so do these muffins with their topping of almonds and sugar. The raspberry filling is an unexpected surprise, something that even the real manna didn't have.

Non-stick butter cooking spray
2 cups flour
2/3 cup sugar
2 teaspoons baking powder
1/2 teaspoon salt
1 cup low-fat buttermilk
2 tablespoons "lite" butter
1/3 cup applesauce
1 egg, slightly beaten
1 teaspoon vanilla
1/2 teaspoon almond extract
5 tablespoons raspberry preserves
4 tablespoons slivered almonds
2 tablespoons sugar

(1) Preheat oven to 400 degrees.
(2) Spray muffin tins.
(3) Lightly spoon flour into measuring cup; level off. In large bowl, combine flour, sugar, baking powder, and salt. Mix well. Add milk, butter, applesauce, egg, vanilla, and almond extract. Stir just until dry ingredients are moistened.
(4) Fill tins 1/2 full. Spoon 1 teaspoon of raspberry preserves into center of batter. Top with 1 tablespoon of batter. Top with almonds and 1 teaspoon sugar in each well.
(5) Bake 12-20 minutes, or until lightly brown. Cool 5 minutes. Remove from tins.

Servings: 12
Calories: 190
Fat (g.): 1.75
Sodium: 47 mg.

The Ten Commandmants

Then God instructed the people as follows:

"I am the Lord your God, who rescued you from slavery in Egypt.

"Do not worship any other gods besides me.

"Do not make idols of any kind, whether in the shape of birds or animals or fish. You must never worship or bow down to them, for I, the Lord God, am a jealous God who will not share your affection with any other god! I do not leave unpunished the sins of those who hate me, but I punish the children for the sins of their parents to the third and fourth generations. But I lavish my love on those who love me and obey my commands, even for a thousand generations.

"Do not misuse the name of the Lord your God. The Lord will not let you go unpunished if you misuse his name.

"Remember to observe the Sabbath day by keeping it holy. Six days a week are set apart for your daily duties and regular work, but the seventh day is a day of rest dedicated to the Lord your God. On that day no one in your household may do any kind of work. This includes you, your sons and daughters, your male and female servants, your livestock, and any foreigners living among you. For in six days the Lord made the heavens, the earth, the sea, and everything in them; then he rested on the seventh day. That is why the Lord blessed the Sabbath day and set it apart as holy.

"Honor your father and mother. Then you will live a long, full life in the land of the Lord your God will give you.

"Do not murder.

"Do not commit adultery.

"Do not steal.

"Do not testify falsely against your neighbor.

"Do not covet your neighbor's house. Do not covet your neighbor's wife, male or female servant, ox or donkey, or anything else your neighbor owns."

When the people heard the thunder and the loud blast of the horn, and when they saw the lightning and the smoke billowing from the mountain, they stood at a distance, trembling with fear.

And they said to Moses, "You tell us what God says, and we will listen. But don't let God speak directly to us. If he does, we will die."

"Don't be afraid," Moses said, "for God has come in this way to show you his awesome power. From now on, let your fear of him keep you from sinning!" *Ex. 20:1-20.*

The first four of the Ten Commandments give us some foundational principles to govern our relationship with God. Of course, the greatest commandment is to "**Love the Lord your God**

with all your heart, all your soul, and all your mind" (Matthew 22:36-38). This includes living out a consistent faith and commitment to Him.

The final six commandments teach principles that define boundaries for healthy human relationships. Jesus summed up these human relational boundaries when he commands: **"Love your neighbor as yourself"** (Matthew 22:39). This command assumes that we have cultivated a healthy self-respect and follow it up with loving actions that respect the boundaries of others.

DID YOU KNOW?

The Greek name of the Ten Commandments is Decalogue, which were written by God on tablets of stone and given to Moses on Mount Sinai.

Ten Vegetables with Pasta

This healthful and hearty dish, with its combination of ten vegetables, will maintain your body as the Ten Commandments maintain your soul.

1 16-ounce package penne rigate
4 cups of assorted vegetables, cut-up:
broccoli; sweet red, yellow, and green peppers; yellow squash; patty pan squash; zucchini; celery; carrots; onion
1/2 cup ripe olives, sliced
1/2 cup fat-free Parmesan cheese, grated
1/3 cup fresh cilantro, chopped
1 cup fat-free Italian salad dressing

(1) Prepare pasta as directed on package; drain. Rinse with cold water; drain.
(2) Mix pasta, vegetables, olives, cheese, and cilantro in large bowl. Add dressing; toss to coat.
(3) Serve immediately or refrigerate until ready to serve.

Servings: 8
Calories: 316
Fat (g.): 1
Sodium: 495 mg.

THREE HOLIDAYS

The Lord commanded the people of Israel to have several religious holidays each year. Three of them were Passover, Harvest Festival, and Tabernacle Festival.

The Lord said to Moses, "Give the Israelites instructions regarding the Lord's appointed festivals, the days when all of you will be summoned to worship me. You may work for six days each week, but on the seventh day all work must come to a complete stop. It is the Lord's Sabbath day of complete rest, a holy day to assemble for worship. It must be observed wherever you live. In addition to the Sabbath, the Lord has established festivals, the holy occasion to be observed at the proper time each year." *Lev. 23:1-4.*

"First comes the Lord's Passover, which begins at twilight on its appointed day in early spring." *Lev. 23:5.* Passover was celebrated to remind the people of the night the Israelites came out of Egypt. That night, the blood of an unblemished lamb was smeared on the two posts and above the door of each Israelite home so the death angel would "pass over" and the first-born male child's life would be spared. The lamb was then roasted whole and eaten by the family. Each year during this event, the people ate a lamb during the night, just as they had done so long ago. Seven days later they ate bread made without yeast. This event was celebrated to remind the people how God punished Pharaoh until he finally set the people of Israel free.

The Harvest Festival happened seven weeks after Passover. It lasted only one day and happened after the grain had been gathered into the barns. God was thanked for sending the rain and the sunshine to make the crops grow and to give them enough food for another year. **"From the day after the Sabbath, the day the bundle of grain was lifted up an offering, count off seven weeks. Keep counting until the day after the seventh Sabbath, fifty days later, and bring an offering of new grain to the Lord. From wherever you live, bring two loaves of bread to be lifted up before the Lord as an offering. These loaves must be baked from three quarts of choice flour that contains yeast. They will be an offering to the Lord from the first of your crops. Along with this bread, present seven one-year-old lambs with no physical defects, one bull, and two rams as burnt offerings to the Lord. These whole burnt offerings, together with the accompanying grain offerings and drink offerings, will be given to the Lord by fire and will be pleasing to him. Then you must offer one male goat as a sin offering and two one-year-old male lambs as a peace offering.**

The Lord will lift up these offerings before the Lord, together with the loaves representing the first of your later crops. These offerings are holy to the Lord and will belong to the priests. That same day, you must stop all your regular work and gather for a sacred assembly. This is a permanent law for you, and it must be observed wherever you live.

When you harvest the crops of your land, do not harvest the grain along the edges of your fields, and do not pick up what the harvesters drop. Leave it for the poor and the foreigners living among you. I, the Lord, am your God." *Lev. 23:15-22.*

The Tabernacle Festival happened at the end of the year. It lasted seven days. During these seven days all the people of Israel moved out of their homes and lived in huts made of branches of trees, just as the Israelites did who lived for forty years while they traveled through the deserts. God wanted them to remember this even when they arrived in Canaan and lived in houses.

At each of these three celebrations every man of Israel was to come bringing a gift to the Lord at the Tabernacle. One gift was olive oil for the seven lamps in the gold lampstand. Another one was finely ground flour to make 12 loaves of bread to place on the gold table near the gold candlestick. The bread was to be put there on the Sabbath and left until the next Sabbath.

DID YOU KNOW?
The Passover was a festival to lay the foundation of Israel's birth as a nation. The Passover speaks of Calvary and of redemption by blood from Egypt, the type of the world, and from Pharaoh, a type of Satan, and from Egyptian servitude, a type of sin. The festival speaks of our redemption from sin by the Lamb of God, Christ being our Passover. The blood of Jesus Christ cleanses His children from all sin.

Lamb, Bread, and Olive Oil

These three holidays of the Old Testament are commemorated by the use of lamb, bread, and olive oil in these two recipes. The marinated lamb makes a delightful alternative to beef in many meat dishes, while the braided bread is an unusual loaf ideal for large groups.

Lamb:

    4 lamb shoulder chops, sliced 1/2" thick
    1/2 cup wine vinegar
    2 tablespoons olive oil
    1/4 cup soy sauce*
    1 tablespoon dill seed

(1) Cut all fat from lamb chops.
(2) Combine vinegar, olive oil, and soy sauce.
(3) Place lamb chops in glass pan.
(4) Pour marinade over meat and marinate at least 3 hours.
(5) 20 minutes before serving: Preheat broiler in oven. When oven is hot (5-10 minutes later), lift chops from marinade and place on broiler pan, sprinkle dill seed on chops. Broil 4-5 minutes on one side. Turn and do the same of the other.

    *May use "lite" soy sauce.
    Note: Barbecuing the lamp chops makes them taste even better.

Braided Bread:

Non-stick vegetable oil cooking spray
3 loaves of frozen bread, thawed
1 egg yolk, beaten
  Sesame seeds
  Poppy seeds

(1) Preheat oven to 375 degrees.
(2) Cut 2 of the 3 loaves of dough in half -- lengthwise. You'll have 4 logs. Spray cookie sheet. Place 3 of the logs together on the cookie sheet and braid them together, pinching close both ends.
(3) Cut the third loaf of dough into thirds -- lengthwise. Place them side by side onto the braid on the cookie sheet. Braid and pinch close both ends.
(4) With the remaining log of dough (step 1), cut into thirds -- lengthwise. Braid and pinch ends like in prior steps.
(5) Brush three-tiered braid with egg and sprinkle seeds generously on top.
(6) Bake about 30 minutes or until golden brown. If top gets too brown, cover with aluminum foil. Cool on wire rack.

Lamb:
Servings: 4
Calories: 155
Fat (g.): 10
Sodium: 1120 mg.

Bread:
Serving: 18
Calories: 376
Fat (g.): 1
Sodium: 1038 mg.

THE YEAR OF JUBILEE

"In addition, you must count off seven Sabbath years, seven years times seven, adding up to forty-nine years in all. Then on the Day of Atonement of the fiftieth year, blow the trumpets loud and long throughout the land. This year will be set apart as holy, a time to proclaim release for all who live there. It will be a jubilee year for you, when each of you returns to the lands that belonged to your ancestors and rejoins your clan. Yes, the fiftieth year will be a jubilee for you. During that year, do not plant any seeds or store away any of the crops that grow naturally, and do not process the grapes that grow on your unpruned vines. It will be a jubilee year for you, and you must observe it as a special and holy time. You may, however, eat the produce that grows naturally in the fields that year. In the Year of Jubilee each of you must return to the lands that belonged to your ancestors."

"When you make an agreement with a neighbor to buy or sell property, you must never take advantage of each other. When you buy land from your neighbor, the price of the land should be based on the number of years since the last jubilee. The seller will charge you only for the crop years left until the next Year of Jubilee. The more the years, the lower the price. After all, the person selling the land is actually selling you a certain number of harvests. Show your fear of God by not taking advantage of each other. I, the Lord, am your God."

"If you want to live securely in the land, keep my laws and obey my regulations. Then the land will yield bumper crops, and you will eat your fill and live securely in it. But you might ask, 'What will we eat during the seventh year, since we are not allowed to plant or harvest crops that year?' The answer is, 'I will order my blessing for you in the sixth year, so the land will produce a bumper crop, enough to support you for three years. As you plant the seed in the eighth year, you will still be eating the produce of the previous year. In fact, you will eat from the old crop until the new harvest comes in the ninth year.' And remember, the land must never be sold on a permanent basis because it really belongs to me. You are only foreigners and tenants living with me." *Lev. 25:8-23.*

In Lev.23:3, the Israelites were commanded to keep a Sabbath -- a day of rest unto the land. Just as the seventh day was designated the Sabbath day, so each seventh year was to be a Sabbath year in which neither sowing nor pruning would occur. What would grow would grow on its own accord. The owner of the land was not to reap what grew up on its own accord during that year. The undressed vine was to be allowed to remain uncut. Instead of the crops being reaped by the owner, they were to provide food for all, rich and poor alike.

After seven Sabbaths of years, 49 years, Israel was to cause the sound of the horn to be heard through the land. The blowing of the horn was to take place on the Day of Atonement, the day that this special year was to begin. The <u>trumpet of the jubilee</u> is literally the horn of shouting. In this fiftieth year, liberty was to be provided to those that had lived without it -- every man would return to his possessions and family. In this year the land would actually belong to the Lord, and not to the individual. It was a glad and happy year. God was to provide large crops the year before so they would have enough to live on during the Sabbath year. If anyone had been so poor that he had to sell the field his father had given him, he got it back free in the year of Jubilee. Or, if anyone had sold himself as a slave, he became free in that year. God told the people if they would obey His commandments, He would send rain so their crops would grow well, luscious fruit would grow on their trees, they would have plenty of bread to eat, and no one would hurt them. The Lord would destroy or drive away any dangerous wild animals. He would take care of his people and make all their enemies afraid of them.

But if they didn't obey His commandments, God said they would have sickness and trouble -- crops would fail, enemies would steal from them, God would send disease and famine, enemies would make war on them.

But if they confessed they had been wicked, and God had punished them, then He wouldn't punish them anymore, but would be kind to them and bring them back again to the land of Canaan.

When the Israelites kept the Lord's commandments, they were to find themselves dwelling in safety -- "security and confidence." The land was to bear enough so they could eat their fill.

DID YOU KNOW?
Jesus is a born-again Christian's jubilee.

Jubilee Chocolate Marble Cheesecake

Chocolate marble cheesecake is a scrumptious dessert reserved for special occasions such as a party, or at any time-- you don't have to wait fifty years to celebrate.

Crust:

1 chocolate or graham cracker prepared pie shell, regular size
2 tablespoons apricot jam, melted

(1) Preheat oven to 350 degrees.
(2) Brush crust with jam, bake for 8 minutes. Remove from oven and cool on rack.

Filling:

1 cup fat-free cottage cheese
4 egg whites or 1 cup fat-free egg substitute
1 cup fat-free ricotta cheese
1 8-ounce package light cream cheese
3/4 cup + 2 tablespoons sugar
1 tablespoon all-purpose flour
1 teaspoon vanilla

1/4 cup unsweetened cocoa powder
1 teaspoon almond extract

(1) Increase oven temperature to 375 degrees.
(2) In a blender or food processor, blend and process cottage cheese until creamy and almost smooth.
(3) Add egg whites and blend until almost smooth.
(4) Add ricotta, cream cheese, 3/4 cup sugar, flour and vanilla. Blend or process until smooth. Transfer half of the filling to a bowl. Stir in the cocoa, remaining 2 tablespoons sugar and almond extract until well blended.
(5) Pour half of each batter mixture into the crust. Then pour the second half of the mixture into the crust. Using a kitchen knife or metal spatula, gently swirl the two batters.
(6) Bake for 35-40 minutes or until a knife inserted in the center comes out clean. Cool on a wire rack until completely cool.
(7) Chill at least 4 hours before serving.

At Holiday Time: Garnish with 3 tablespoons fat-free cream, 1 teaspoon chopped nuts, and a cherry (per serving).

Servings: 10
Calories: 254
Fat (g.): 6 (without addition of nuts)
Sodium: 379 mg.

JERICHO'S WALLS FALL DOWN

While the Israelites were camped at Gilgal on the plains of Jericho, they celebrated Passover on the evening of the fourteenth day of the first month -- the month that marked their exodus from Egypt. The very next day they began to eat unleavened bread and roasted grain harvested from the land. No manna appeared that day, and it was never seen again. So from that time on the Israelites ate from the crops of Canaan.

As Joshua approached the city of Jericho, he looked up and saw a man facing him with sword in hand. Joshua went up to him and asked, "Are you friend or foe?"

"Neither one," he replied. "I am commander of the Lord's army."

At this, Joshua fell with his face to the ground in reverence. "I am at your command," Joshua said. "What do you want your servant to do?"

The commander of the Lord's army replied, "Take off your sandals, for this is holy ground." And Joshua did as he was told.

Now the gates of Jericho were tightly shut because the people were afraid of the Israelites. No one was allowed to go in or out. But the Lord said to Joshua, "I have given you Jericho, its king, and all its mighty warriors. Your entire army is to march around the city once a day for six days. Seven priests will walk ahead of the Ark, each carrying a ram's horn. On the seventh day you are to march around the city seven times, with the priests blowing the horns. When you hear the priests give one long blast on the horns, have all the people give a mighty shout. Then the walls of the city will collapse, and the people can charge straight into the city." *Josh. 5:10-15 -- 6:1-5.*

Joshua did what the Lord had commanded him. On the seventh day the Israelites marched around Jericho seven times. The priests sounded the blast on their horns. **When the people heard the sound of the horns, they shouted as loud as they could. Suddenly, the walls of Jericho collapsed, and the Israelites charged straight into the city from every side and captured it. They completely destroyed everything in it -- men and women, young and old, sheep, donkeys -- everything.** *Josh. 6:20-21.*

DID YOU KNOW?

The ark of the covenant that followed Joshua and his army around the walls of Jericho symbolized to Israel that Jehovah was with them and leading them in this strange maneuver. We see the trumpet of faith in this story. Israel was doing God's work in His way, no matter how foolish the marching must have seemed.

Jericho's Walls Fall Down Enchiladas

Joshua's army would have loved these tasty but low-fat enchiladas. When you eat them, you'll want to blow your trumpet, too!

12 corn or fat-free flour tortillas
3 large chicken breasts, baked and diced
1 28-ounce can enchilada sauce
1 large onion, chopped
3/4 cup fat-free cheddar cheese
3 large garlic cloves, minced
1 teaspoon cumin
1 28-ounce can fat-free zesty jalapeno refried beans

(1) Preheat oven to 400 degrees.
(2) Pour 1/3 of enchilada sauce into bottom of 2 large baking pans.
(3) Mix in medium sized bowl -- chicken, onion, garlic, 1/2 cup cheese, and cumin.
(4) In a large frying pan warm rest of enchilada sauce and dip tortillas, one by one, in the sauce and then into pan. Place 3 tablespoons of chicken mixture, and 2 tablespoons of beans, into each tortilla and fold over. Press down firmly.
(5) When all enchiladas have been made, pour remaining enchilada sauce over enchiladas. Sprinkle with remaining cheese.
(6) Cover tightly with aluminum foil and bake for 30-35 minutes.

Servings: 6
Calories: 466
Fat (g.): 2
Sodium: 1088 mg.

ALMOST THERE

The people of Israel wandered around in the wilderness for forty long years. God wouldn't let them go into the Promised Land of Canaan because they had refused to do what God had told them to do. They had listened to the ten spies who were afraid. So God said they must all die in the wilderness. Only the children, Caleb, and Joshua could go into the Promised Land!

The Lord led the Israelites to the river Jordan and waited for Moses to tell them to cross. The Lord told Moses that the Israelites must drive out all the heathen nations living across the river. They must destroy all their idols and break down all the heathen altars they would find there so they would not be tempted to worship those idols. If they obeyed God, every Israelite family would be given enough land for home and farm.

While they (the Israelites) **were camped near the Jordan River on the plains of Moab opposite Jericho, the Lord said to Moses, "Speak to the Israelites and tell them: 'When you cross the Jordan River into the land of Canaan, you must drive out all the people living there. You must destroy all their carved and molten images and demolish all their pagan shrines. Take possession of the land and settle in it, because I have given it to you to occupy. You must distribute the land among the clans by sacred lot and in proportion to their size. A large inheritance of land will be allotted to each of the larger clans, and a smaller inheritance will be allotted to each of the smaller clans. The decision of the sacred lot is final. In this way, the land will be divided among your ancestral tribes. But if you fail to drive out the people who live in the land, those who remain will be like splinters in your eyes and thorns in your sides. They will harass you in the land where you live. And I will do to you what I had planned to do to them.'"** *Num. 33:50-56.*

When the ten spies returned from the Promised Land and gave a negative report, it showed that their understanding of God was limited by their weak faith. Instead of surrendering their lives to God as responsible men and women, they rebelled and refused to accept his right to rule over them. They were unable to see the truth because they were looking to their own strength, not God's. Because of that tragic decision a whole generation of people, except Joshua and Caleb and the children, perished in the desert.

Many times it is in our personal wilderness experience that we find the true meaning of life, faith, and a personal relationship with God. Once we have truly found it we treasure it above all else. God graciously cleanses us and forgives us, but it requires personal responsibility to stay in the Promised Land. As we act on God's promises and follow the plan he has set for us, we enjoy "joy unspeakable and full of power."

DID YOU KNOW?

Three important principles can be learned from the life of Joshua: (1) what we think about God has a powerful effect on what we do, (2) since Adam's fall, people have had to endure pain whether they accept responsibility or not, and (3) our decision on whether or not to accept responsibility many times determines the type of pain we experience and the effect it will have on us.

Almost There Baked Beans

It took a long time for God's people to reach the Promised Land, and it takes a long time for this recipe to cook. However, you won't have to wait forty years to enjoy the rich, hearty taste of these baked beans.

Non-stick vegetable oil cooking spray
1/2 medium onion, chopped
1 cup, very low-fat turkey sausage, diced
4 ounces ground turkey (10% fat or less)
2 16-ounce cans chili beans
1 16-ounce can red kidney beans, rinsed and drained
1/2 cup tomato sauce
1/2 tablespoon brown sugar
1-2 teaspoon liquid smoke
1/2 teaspoon maple flavoring

(1) Lightly spray an unheated medium-sized skillet with spray. Add the onions and sausage. Cook and stir over medium-high heat until the onions are tender. Add the turkey and cook until browned, stirring occasionally.

(2) Transfer the onion mixture to a 4-6 quart crockpot. Stir in the chili beans, kidney beans, tomato sauce, brown sugar, liquid smoke, and maple flavoring. Cover and cook on the medium-high heat setting 4-6 hours. Stir before serving.

Servings: 6
Calories: 193
Fat (g.): 1
Sodium: 1523 mg.

LONG JOURNEY ENDS

Joshua and his troops won many battles against many kings, but there was still much land that needed to be conquered.

All the people of Israel went to the city of Shiloh to permanently set up the Tabernacle. The people had grown tired of war and wanted rest and quiet. It seemed the people did not want all the good land God was willing to give them.

Joshua asked the people to choose 21 scouts to inspect all the unconquered land. The scouts wrote out their report and gave it to Joshua.

Joshua drew straws for the different tribes of Israel so the Lord could tell them which part of the land they should have. God told them to finish driving out the heathen nations and He would help His people do this.

The priests and Levites were not to own farms but to stay at the Tabernacle and work for God there. God said the rest of the people could have cities of their own in which to live.

These are Joshua's final words to Israel. **"I am an old man now. You have seen everything the Lord your God has done for you during my lifetime. The Lord your God has fought for you against your enemies. I have allotted to you as an inheritance all the land of the nations yet unconquered, as well as the land of those we have already conquered -- from the Jordan River to the Mediterranean Sea in the west. This land will be yours, for the Lord your God will drive out all the people living there now. You will live there instead of them, just as the Lord your God promised you."**

"So be strong! Be very careful to follow all the instructions written in the Book of the Law of Moses. Do not deviate from them in any way. Make sure you do not associate with the other people still remaining in the land. Do not even mention the names of their gods, much less swear by them or worship them. But be faithful to the Lord your God as you have done until now."

"For the Lord has driven out great and powerful nations for you, and no one has yet been able to defeat you. Each one of you will put to flight a thousand of the enemy, for the Lord your God fights for you, just as he has promised. So be very careful to love the Lord your God."

"But if you turn away from him and intermarry with the survivors of these nations remaining among you, then know for certain that the Lord your God will no longer drive them out from your land. Instead, they will be a snare and a trap to you, a pain in your side

and a thorn in your eyes, and you will be wiped out from this good land the Lord your God has given you."

"Soon I will die, going the way of all the earth. Deep in your hearts you know that every promise of the Lord your God has come true. Not a single one has failed. But as surely as the Lord your God has given you the good things he promised, he will also bring disaster on you if you disobey him. He will completely wipe you out from this good land he has given you. If you break the covenant of the Lord your God by worshipping and serving other gods, his anger will burn against you, and you will quickly be wiped out from the good land he has given you." *Josh. 23:2b-16.*

DID YOU KNOW?
Joshua reminded the children of Israel that God had given them all their victories, that the land of Canaan was apportioned as God had said it would be, and He would continue to defeat Israel's enemies so his people could live in peace.

Journey Cake Plus

At the end of the Exodus, the Israelites moved into Canaan with its fertile fields and good crops. These cakes, simple cornbread spiced with the addition of zesty ingredients, symbolize the abundance of good food now available to the Israelites.

Non-stick vegetable oil cooking spray
3 zucchini, quartered and thinly sliced
1/2 sweet red bell pepper, diced
1/2 cup onion, chopped
1/2 cup evaporated skim milk
3/4 cup of egg substitute or 3 egg whites
1 8-ounce package corn muffin mix
3/4 cup finely shredded fat-reduced sharp cheddar cheese

(1) Preheat oven to 375 degrees. Lightly spray an unheated large skillet with cooking spray. Add zucchini, pepper, and onions. Cook and stir over medium-high heat until zucchini is crisp-tender. Remove from the heat and set aside.
(2) Lightly spray a 9" pie plate.
(3) In a large bowl beat together milk and egg whites. Stir in the muffin mix just until combined. Then fold in the zucchini mixture and 1/2 cup of the cheese.
(4) Transfer the mixture to the prepared pie plate. Sprinkle with remaining cheese. Bake 35-40 minutes until golden brown and a toothpick inserted into the center comes out clean.

Servings: 8
Calories: 196
Fat (g.): 4
Sodium: 448 mg.

GOD KEEPS ON HELPING HIS PEOPLE

The angel of the Lord went up from Gilgal to Bokim with a message for the Israelites. He told them, "I brought you out of Egypt into this land that I swore to give your ancestors, and I said I would never break my covenant with you. For your part, you were not to make any covenants with the people living in this land, instead, you were to destroy their altars. Why, then, have you disobeyed my command? Since you have done this, I will no longer drive out the people living in your land. They will be thorns in your sides, and their gods will be a constant temptation to you." When the angel of the Lord finished speaking, the Israelites wept loudly. So they called the place "Weeping," and they offered sacrifices to the Lord. *Judges 2:1-5.*

After Joshua's death, the Israelite army continued to fight the heathen nations as God had told them to. God helped them and made them victorious, but they stopped fighting before they had driven out all the nations of Canaan. Some heathen nations stayed.

When Israelites turned away from idols and again asked the Lord to help them, He helped them by raising up judges. These men helped them fight against their masters and win. The Lord would set the people free, the people would forget the Lord and sin again by worshipping idols, ignoring the Lord. The process of sinning and repenting went on for more than 30 years.

After the generation died, another generation grew up who did not acknowledge the Lord or remember the mighty things he had done for Israel. Then the Israelites did what was evil in the Lord's sight and worshipped the images of Baal. They abandoned the Lord, the God of their ancestors, who had brought them out of Egypt. They chased after other gods, worshipping the gods of the people around them. And they angered the Lord. They abandoned the Lord to serve Baal and the images of Ashtoreth. This made the Lord burn with anger against Israel, so he handed them over to marauders who stole their possessions. He sold them to their enemies all around, and they were no longer able to resist them. Every time Israel went out to battle, the Lord fought against them. *Judges 2:10-15a.*

DID YOU KNOW?
The generations of Joshua and his immediate successors remained true to the Lord because of their association with the great works of the Lord.

Mixed Up Meatballs

God keeps helping His people despite them becoming mixed up in following His plans. These meatballs may be "mixed-up," but they provide wonderful nutrition and taste.

1-1/2 pounds lean ground turkey (10% or less fat)

1/2 cup unseasoned dry bread crumbs
1/3 cup onion, minced
1/4 cup cilantro, chopped
1 egg white
1/2 teaspoon each garlic powder and ground sage
1/4 teaspoon each salt and freshly ground black pepper
1 cup seedless raspberry jam
1/4 cup prepared mustard
1-1/2 tablespoons prepared horseradish

(1) Combine ground turkey, bread crumbs, onion, cilantro, egg white, garlic powder, sage, salt, pepper in a medium bowl. Mix well (hands work best). Form mixture into bite-size meatballs, about 1-inch in diameter.

(2) Place meatballs on a large baking sheet that has been sprayed with non-stick spray. Bake at 400 degrees for 12-15 minutes, until cooked through (test for doneness after 12 minutes). Remove from oven and transfer to a large saucepan.

(3) In a small saucepan, stir together jam, mustard, and horseradish. Cook over medium-high heat for 2-3 minutes, stirring often. Sauce will be thick and bubbly. Pour sauce over meatballs. Stir well. Cover and simmer over low heat for 10 minutes. Transfer to a serving dish and serve hot. Can be served over rice.

Servings: 8
Calories: 233
Fat (g.): 1.8
Sodium: 307 mg.

VISIT FROM AN ANGEL

Again the Israelites did what was evil in the Lord's sight. So the Lord handed them over to the Midianites for seven years. The Midianites were so cruel that the Israelites fled to the mountains, where they made hiding places for themselves in caves and dens. *Judges 6:1.*

When they cried out to the Lord because of Midian, the Lord sent a prophet to the Israelites. He said, "This is what the Lord, the God of Israel, says: I brought you up out of slavery in Egypt and rescued you from the Egyptians and from all who oppressed you. I drove out your enemies and gave you their land. I told you, 'I am the Lord your God. You must not worship the gods of the Amorites, in whose land you now live.' But you have not listened to me."

Then the angel of the Lord came and sat beneath the oak tree at Ophrah, which belonged to Joash of the clan of Abiezer. Gideon, son of Joash, had been threshing wheat at the bottom of a winepress to hide the grain from the Midianites. The angel of the Lord appeared to him and said, "Mighty hero, the Lord is with you!"

"Sir," Gideon replied, "if the Lord is with us, why has all this happened to us? And where are all the miracles our ancestors told us about? Didn't they say, 'The Lord brought us up out of Egypt?' But now the Lord has abandoned us and handed us over to the Midianites."

Then the Lord turned to him and said, "Go with the strength you have and rescue Israel from the Midianites. I am sending you!"

"But Lord," Gideon replied, "How can I rescue Israel? My clan is the weakest in the whole tribe of Manasseh, and I am the least in my entire family!"

The Lord said to him, "I will be with you. And you will destroy the Midianites as if you were fighting against one man."

Gideon replied, "If you are truly going to help me, show me a sign to prove that it is really the Lord speaking to me. Don't go away until I come back and bring my offering to you."

The Lord answered, "I will stay here until you return."

Gideon hurried home. He cooked a young goat, and with half a bushel of flour he baked some bread without yeast. Then, carrying the meat in a basket and the broth in a pot, he brought them out and presented them to the angel, who was under the oak tree.

The angel of God said to him, "Place the meat and the unleavened bread on this rock, and pour the broth over it." And Gideon did as he was told. Then the angel of the Lord touched the meat and bread with the staff in his hand, and fire flamed up from the rock and consumed all he had brought. And the angel of the Lord disappeared.

When Gideon realized that it was the angel of the Lord, he cried out, "Sovereign Lord, I have seen the angel of the Lord face to face!"

"It is all right," the Lord replied. "Do not be afraid. You will not die." And Gideon built an altar to the Lord there and named it "The Lord is Peace." *Judges 6:7-24a.*

Gideon responded to the message from the angel with little hope or faith. He was so used to oppression by the Midianites that he had little hope that anything could change. He saw himself as weak and unimportant and viewed God as one who could not be trusted to do miracles. When we try to do things in our own power in the midst of terrible circumstances we can easily become worn down by the continual pain of not being able to break free. Facing the situation honestly is an important first step. When we are willing to speak the truth about the situation then we are ready to see that God *can* deliver us from it.

Gideon's hesitant response may have come from his family's poverty and his position in his family. God offered his power to Gideon as a means to help him overcome his own sense of inadequacy. God often has great tasks he has planned for us to accomplish. As we confess our inadequacy, He will make us more than adequate by His power. As we trust him He says He will be with us to carry out whatever tasks He has assigned to us.

DID YOU KNOW?
In times of trouble we often search for spectacular evidences of God's direction in our lives. The truth is that God often reveals the answers in our hearts.

Visit From An Angel Food Cake

Take one bite of this spectacular angel food cake and you will think you've been visited by an angel.

1 cup <u>each</u> strawberries, raspberries, and blueberries (if using frozen berries, buy the unsweetened variety and thaw before using)
1 tablespoon sugar
3/4 cup fat-free sour cream
3 tablespoons honey
1 tablespoon frozen orange juice concentrate
1 angel food cake, store-bought or made from a mix

Topping:

(1) Combine berries and sugar in a medium bowl. Combine and refrigerate until serving time. Combine sour cream, honey, and orange juice concentrate in a small bowl. Cover and refrigerate.

Cake:

(1) If baked, cool by inverting onto the neck of a bottle about 1-1/2 hours.

Assembly:

(1) Place cake on footed cake plate, if possible. Top each slice with 2-3 tablespoons berries. Drizzle with 1-2 tablespoons of orange cream sauce.

Servings: 12
Calories: 148
Fat (g.): 0
Sodium: 146 mg.

A BEAUTIFUL LOVE STORY

In the days when the judges ruled in Israel, a man from Bethlehem in Judah left the country because of a severe famine. He took his wife and two sons and went to live in the country of Moab. The man's name was Elimelech, and his wife was Naomi. Their two sons were Mahlon and Kilion. During their stay in Moab, Elimelech died and Naomi was left with her two sons. The two sons married Moabite women. One married a woman named Orpah, and the other a woman named Ruth. But about ten years later, both Mahlon and Kilion died. This left Naomi alone, without her husband or sons. *Ruth 1:1-2a,3-4.*

Then Naomi heard in Moab that the Lord had blessed his people in Judah by giving them good crops again. So Naomi and her daughters-in-law got ready to leave Moab to return to her homeland. With her two daughters-in-law she set out from the place where she had been living, and they took the road that would lead them back to Judah.

But on the way, Naomi said to her two daughters-in-law, "Go back to your mothers' homes instead of coming with me. And may the Lord reward you for your kindness to your husbands and to me. May the Lord bless you with the security of another marriage." Then she kissed them good-bye, and they all broke down and wept.

"No," they said. "We want to go with you to your people."

"But," Naomi replied, "Why should you go on with me? Can I still give birth to other sons who could grow up to be your husbands?" *Ruth 1:6-11.*

And again they wept together, and Orpah kissed her mother-in-law good-bye. But Ruth insisted on staying with Naomi.

But Ruth replied, "Don't ask me to leave you and turn back. I will go wherever you go and live wherever you live. Your people will be my people, and your God will be my God. I will die where you die and will be buried there. May the Lord punish me severely if I allow anything but death to separate us!" *Ruth 1:14,16-18.*

Now there was a wealthy and influential man in Bethlehem named Boaz, who was a relative of Naomi's husband, Elimelech. *Ruth 2:1*

One day Naomi said to Ruth, "My daughter, it's time that I found a permanent home for you, so that you will be provided for. Boaz is a close relative of ours, and he's been very kind by letting you gather grain with his workers. Tonight he will be winnowing barley at the threshing floor. Now do all I tell you -- take a bath and put on perfume and dress in your nicest clothes. Then go to the threshing floor, but don't let Boaz see you until he has finished his meal. Be sure to notice where he lies down; then go and uncover his feet and lie down there. He will tell you what to do." *Ruth 3:1-4.*

After Boaz had finished his meal and was in good spirits, he lay down beside the heap of grain and went to sleep. Then Ruth came quietly, uncovered his feet, and lay down. Around midnight, Boaz suddenly woke up and turned over. He was surprised to find a woman lying at his feet! "Who are you?" he demanded.

"I am your servant Ruth," she replied. "Spread the corner of your covering over me, for you are my family redeemer."

"The Lord bless you, my daughter!" Boaz exclaimed. "You are showing more family loyalty now than ever by not running after a younger man, whether rich or poor. Now don't worry about a thing, my daughter. I will do what is necessary, for everyone in town knows you are an honorable woman. But there is one problem. While it is true that I am one of your family redeemers, there is another man who is more closely related to you than I am. Stay here tonight, and in the morning I will talk to him." *Ruth 3:7-11.*

So Boaz went to the town gate and took a seat there. When the family redeemer he had mentioned came by, Boaz called out to him, "Come over here, friend. I want to talk with you." *Ruth 4:1a.* They sat and talked. The man chose not to act as Ruth's kinsmen redeemer and purchase the land that had belonged to Naomi's husband. If he purchased the land he would have to marry Ruth, too. The man declined the offer. So Boaz was free to purchase the land and marry Ruth.

Then Boaz said to the leaders and to the crowd standing around, "You are witnesses that today I have bought from Naomi all the property of Elimelech, Kilion, and Mahlon. And with the land I have acquired Ruth, the Moabite widow of Mahlon, to be my wife." *Ruth 9:10a.*

Then the leaders and all the people standing there replied, "We are witnesses! May the Lord make the woman who is now coming into your home like Rachel and Leah, from whom all the nation of Israel descended! May you be great in Ephrathah and famous in Bethlehem. And may the Lord give you descendants by this young woman who will be like those of our ancestor Perez, the son of Tamar and Judah." *Ruth 4:11-12.*

The story of Ruth and Naomi is a beautiful story of two lives woven together by grief, grace, and spiritual friendship that would one day give rise to the lineage of Israel's greatest king and the Messiah.

Ruth's newfound faith in Jehovah and her love for Naomi were cultivated by her discipline of service. Ruth served Naomi by gladly gleaning the fields for food. As Ruth served, God guided her to where she could be richly blessed.

In Ruth's relationship with Naomi, she also practiced the discipline of spiritual friendship. This discipline worked in both their lives and helped them grow closer to God in several ways.

First, Naomi acted as a valuable role model for Ruth to grow and mature in her relationship with God. Second, they were able to help each other as they healed from the wounds of life. Third, their friendship opened the way to a new and better future.

DID YOU KNOW?

God's second greatest commandment requires that we love our neighbor as ourselves. As we love others, we love ourselves in turn as well as showing our love for the Lord. Also, by blessing others, we receive blessing. This is the kind of love that allows God's love to be visible to the world.

Love Story Chocolate Cream Pie

This is a beautiful dessert for a beautiful love story.

<u>Crust</u>:

    Non-stick vegetable oil cooking spray
    1-1/2 cups crushed chocolate graham crust
    1 egg white

(1) Preheat oven to 375 degrees.
(2) In a medium bowl, stir together crumbs and egg white until well-blended. Spray a 9-inch pie plate with non-stick spray. Press crumb mixture on bottom and up sides of pie plate. Bake for 8 minutes. Let cool before filling.

<u>Filling</u>:

    2 envelopes whipped topping mix
    2-3/4 cups fat-free <u>cold</u> milk, divided
    2 packages (4-serving size) <u>instant</u> chocolate pudding and pie filling

(1) Beat whipped topping mix and 1 cup milk in large bowl with electric mixer on high speed 6 minutes or until topping thickens and form peaks.
(2) Add remaining milk and pie filling mixes; beat on low speed until blended. Beat on high 2 minutes, scraping bowl occasionally.
(3) Spoon into pie crust. Refrigerate at least 4 hours.

Note: Can be decorated with non-fat dairy topping, maraschino cherries, mini chocolate chips, finely chopped nuts or peanuts.

Servings: 8
Calories: 203 (without addition of chocolate chips or nuts)
Fat (g.): 1.9
Sodium: 401 mg.

DAVID KILLS A GIANT

Once again the Philistine army decided to fight Israel, and Saul and the men of Israel got ready for the battle. One of the Philistine soldiers was a giant named Goliath. He was very boastful. Saul and the men of Israel were frightened. No one in his army was willing to fight the giant. For forty days Goliath came out every morning and evening to defy the men of Israel.

Meanwhile, a shepherd boy named David was told to visit his brothers in Saul's army, to take them food and see how they were doing.

As David was visiting his brothers, Goliath strutted out and gave his usual taunt. "How dare this giant defy the armies of the living God?" demanded David. After giving Saul some assurance that he could fight the giant, David went out to meet him. David chose five smooth stones from a brook, put them into his shepherd's bag, took his stick with him that he used to protect his sheep, and his slingshot. He rushed out to fight. Goliath jeered at him. But David said, **"You come to me with sword, spear, and javelin, but I come to you in the name of the Lord Almighty -- the God of the armies of Israel, whom you have defied. Today the Lord will conquer you, and I will kill you and cut off your head. And then I will give the dead bodies of your men to the birds and wild animals, and the whole world will know that there is a God in Israel! And everyone will know that the Lord does not need weapons to rescue his people. It is his battle, not ours. The Lord will give you to us!"** *I Samuel 17:45-47.* That's exactly what happened.

DID YOU KNOW?
When being confronted by the giant, Goliath, the Israelite soldiers saw some of the truth -- their limitations -- and ran away. David truthfully acknowledged his limitations but knew the power of God. That knowledge of God gave him the courage he needed to do what was needed. The whole truth is -- we can't overcome alone, yet because God is very powerful and eager to help us, we can do whatever He has called us to do.

Giant-Size Pizza Pie

You, too, will feel as if you've slain a giant when you and your friends have finished this huge pizza pie.

Filling:

1 pound ground turkey (10% or less fat)
1 cup onion, chopped
2 cloves garlic, minced

8-ounce can tomato sauce
1.25-ounce envelope taco seasoning mix

(1) Heat oven to 425 degrees.
(2) In a large skillet, brown ground turkey, onion, and garlic. Stir in tomato sauce and taco seasoning mix. Simmer 5 minutes.

Crust:

1 large store-bought pizza crust or equivalent (follow package directions)

(1) Prepare pizza crust according to package directions, if applicable. Bake according to package directions. Remove from oven.

Assembly:

4 ounces reduced-fat cheddar cheese, shredded
1-1/2 cups lettuce, shredded
1 cup tomatoes, chopped
1 cup scallions, sliced
1/4 cup black olives, slices
1/2 small avocado, sliced
1/2 cup non-fat sour cream

(1) Spread meat mixture over baked pizza crust. Bake at 425 degrees for 10-12 minutes. Remove from oven.
(2) Arrange shredded lettuce around sides and top of crust to resemble "hair." Place all but 2 olives slices around green hair. Place one slice of avocado on each side about half way down to resemble "ears." Place two dollops of sour cream in eye areas and one slice of olive in center to resemble "eyes." Place a triangle of chopped tomato to resemble a "nose." Place an upside-down moon-shaped wedge of chopped tomato to resemble a "sad" mouth.

Servings: 8
Calories: 180
Fat (g.): 2.5
Sodium: 771 mg.

KING DAVID

David was at home in Ziklag when a messenger arrived from the battlefield to tell him that Saul, the king, and Saul's son, Jonathan, were dead.

The young man told David that Saul had commanded him to kill the king before Saul's enemies could. He told David he had killed the king. It was a lie; Saul killed himself with his own sword. David was very angry at the young man and ordered him killed.

David asked God if he should go to the land of Israel. God told him to go to the land of Hebron (one of the cities of the tribe of Judah, to which David belonged).

Upon David's arrival at Hebron, the leaders asked him to be their king. He accepted. Years before, God had told Samuel to anoint David as the future king of Israel. The other tribes did not come to David because they had a king, Ishbosheth, a son of Saul. One day while the king, Ishbosheth, was taking a nap two of his captains came into his room and killed him. They cut off his head and bought it to David. David was furious and reminded them he had executed the man he thought had killed King Saul. He had these two captains executed, also. When the tribes saw that their king, Ishbosheth, was dead they asked David to be their king, too. Now David was king over all the twelve tribes of Israel.

David was a very great man for God. The Lord helped him in everything he did.

Then all the tribes of Israel went to David at Hebron and told him, "We are all members of your family. For a long time, even while Saul was our king, you were the one who really led Israel. And the Lord has told you, 'You will be the shepherd of my people Israel. You will be their leader.'" *II Samuel 5:1-3.*

The secret to David's success was that he acknowledged God as his source in everything he did. If we take the credit for our success, it is an indication that we are not living a fully surrendered life to God at that moment. As we praise God for the victories, we show Him how much we love Him and how much we appreciate His help.

DID YOU KNOW?
The only deep mourning for Saul, the king before David, was by David, the person Saul had hated the most and persecuted for so many years, even up to the time of his death.

King David's Beef Stew

Here's a hearty beef stew fit for a king. If it had actually existed in David's time, he might have written a psalm mentioning it.

Non-stick vegetable or butter oil cooking spray
1/4 cup all-purpose flour
1/2 teaspoon freshly ground black pepper
1 pound, extra lean, stew beef, trimmed of all visible fat and cut into 1/2-inch cubes
1 cup non-alcoholic red wine
1 cup small pearl onions
1 cup carrots, sliced
1 cup potatoes, peeled and cubed
2 cloves garlic, minced
2 bay leaves
1/4 teaspoon dried thyme
1 can (14-1/2 ounces) beef broth
2 tablespoons Worcestershire sauce
1-1/2 cups mushrooms, sliced
1/2 cup <u>frozen</u> green peas
2 tablespoons cornstarch
1/4 teaspoon salt
1/4 teaspoon freshly ground pepper

(1) In medium bowl, combine flour and 1/4 teaspoon pepper. Using clean hands, add beef and toss to thoroughly coat with seasoned flour. Shake off any excess flour.
(2) Spray large frying pan and heat over medium-high heat. Add half the beef and cook, stirring constantly, 5 minutes or until beef is browned. Remove browned beef and set aside. Spray pan again, brown remaining beef. Leave in pan.
(3) To pan, add a little wine. Stir with wooden spoon to loosen any browned bits stuck to bottom. Return first batch of browned beef to second batch in fry pan. Add onions, carrots, potatoes, garlic, bay leaves, thyme, remaining wine, Worcestershire sauce, and beef broth.
(4) Partially cover and bring to a boil over medium heat. Simmer gently over low heat about 50 minutes or until beef is tender when pierced with a fork.
(5) Add mushrooms. Cook 5 minutes. Add peas and cook 5 minutes more.
(6) Place 1/2 cup of broth in a small bowl. Add cornstarch and stir to dissolve. Add cornstarch mixture to stew. Stir over medium heat until gravy thickens. Add salt and pepper. Remove and discard bay leaves.

Calories: 8
Servings: 219
Fat (g.): 2
Sodium: 209 mg.

GOD'S BEAUTIFUL TEMPLE

Solomon feared God, and was careful to do what was right. One night God spoke to him in a dream telling him he could have anything he wanted. Solomon decided to ask for wisdom. He wanted God to guide him to do what was best for his people. Because Solomon asked for something that would bless his people and not just himself, God gave Solomon riches besides. With wisdom and riches, Solomon was now ready to build God's Temple.

He carefully followed the pattern his father David had given him.

It was in mid-spring, during the fourth year of Solomon's reign, that he began the construction of the Temple of the Lord. This was 480 years after the people of Israel were delivered from their slavery in the land of Egypt.

The Temple that King Solomon built for the Lord was 90 feet long, 30 feet wide, and 45 feet high. The foyer at the front of the Temple was 30 feet wide, running across the entire width of the Temple. It projected outward 15 feet from the front of the Temple. Solomon also made narrow, recessed windows throughout the Temple. *I Kings 6:1-4.*

Then the Lord gave this message to Solomon: "Concerning this Temple you are building, if you keep all my laws and regulations and obey all my commands, I will fulfill through you the promise I made to your father, David. I will live among the people of Israel and never forsake my people." *I Kings 6:11,12.*

One great quality Solomon possessed was his willingness to share his knowledge with others. He could have been very egotistical but he chose not to be. People came from all over to listen and learn from the wisdom God gave to Solomon.

King David, Solomon's father, had established a strong relationship with Hiram of Tyre. Solomon continued that relationship and enjoyed the benefits of doing so. Hiram availed himself to provide expertise and numerous materials for building the Temple that Solomon needed.

DID YOU KNOW?
When Solomon was building the Temple he set up shifts of one month at work and two months at home. Obviously, Solomon placed great importance on the family.

Layered Temple Salad with Light and Creamy Parmesan Dressing

Israel's wisest king might have chosen this magnificent salad to serve at the feast dedicating the new Temple.

Layered Salad

4 cups torn lettuce*
1 cup fresh mushroom, sliced
1 10-ounce package of peas, frozen
1 cup radishes, sliced
1 cup zucchini, sliced
1 cup yellow crookneck squash, diced
4 cups hard cooked egg whites, chopped (discard yolks)
5 slices turkey bacon, cooked, drained, and crumbled
1/2 cup fat-free cheddar cheese
1-1/2 cups Creamy Parmesan dressing
1/4 cup scallions, sliced

(1) Place lettuce in a large clear glass bowl with straight sides. In the following order, layer the mushrooms, peas, carrots, radishes, zucchini, yellow squash, egg whites and turkey bacon on top. Sprinkle with 1/4 cup of the cheddar cheese. Carefully spread the dressing over the top, sealing the dressing to the edge of the bowl. Sprinkle with the remaining 1/4 cup cheddar cheese and scallions. Cover and refrigerate 24 hours.
(2) To serve, toss the salad until the lettuce and vegetables are coated.

*I suggest a mix of greens - romaine, red leaf, curly leaf, raddichio, etc.

Light and Creamy Parmesan Dressing:

1 cup fat-free plain yogurt
1 cup fat-free sour cream
1 cup fat-free Parmesan cheese, grated
4 tablelspoons fresh lemon juice
2 cloves garlic, minced
Freshly ground pepper

(1) In a small bowl, use a wire whisk to stir together all ingredients except black pepper. Cover and chill in the refrigerator for at least 30 minutes.
(2) Before serving, sprinkle with ground pepper. Toss.

Salad:
Servings: 8
Calories:123
Fat (g.): 4
Sodium: 410 mg.

Dressing:
Servings: 8
Calories: 48
Fat (g.): 1.5
Sodium: 48 mg.

ELIJAH'S PICNIC

Now Elijah, who was from Tishbe in Gilead, told King Ahab, "As surely as the Lord, the God of Israel, lives -- the God whom I worship and serve -- there will be no dew or rain during the next few years unless I give the word!"

Then the Lord said to Elijah, "Go to the east and hide by Kerith Brook at a place east of where it enters the Jordan River. Drink from the brook and eat what the ravens bring you, for I have commanded them to bring you food."

So Elijah did as the Lord had told him and camped beside Kerith Brook. The ravens brought him bread and meat each morning and evening, and he drank from the brook. But after a while the brook dried up, for there was no rainfall anywhere in the land.

Then the Lord said to Elijah, "Go and live in the village of Zarephath, near the city of Sidon. There is a widow there who will feed you. I have given her my instructions."

So he went to Zarephath. As he arrived at the gates of the village, he saw a widow gathering sticks, and he asked her, "Would you please bring me a cup of water?" As she was going to get it, he called to her, "Bring me a bite of bread, too."

But she said, "I swear by the Lord your God that I don't have a single piece of bread in the house. And I have only a handful of flour left in the jar and a little cooking oil in the bottom of the jug. I was just gathering a few sticks to cook this last meal, and then my son and I will die."

But Elijah said to her, "Don't be afraid! Go ahead and cook that 'last meal,' but bake me a little loaf of bread first. Afterward there will still be enough food for you and your son. For this is what the Lord, the God of Israel, says: There will always be plenty of flour and oil left in your containers until the time when the Lord sends rain and the crops grow again!"

So she did as Elijah said, and she and Elijah and her son continued to eat from her supply of flour and oil for many days. For no matter how much they used, there was always enough left in the containers, just as the Lord had promised through Elijah. *I Kings 17:1-16.*

The widow of Zarephath demonstrated great faith in God's ability to provide for her needs. She and her son faced starvation, yet she still chose to trust God. That complete trust in God resulted in her deliverance. God provided for her need. Once again, God provided for her and took care of her because she was willing to trust Him.

DID YOU KNOW?

Elijah's time in the wilderness forced him to practice three very important spiritual disciplines that freed him from dependence on the world and its lusts and encouraged him to trust completely in God. These disciplines were: (1) solitude, (2) silence, and (3) fasting.

Picnic Olive Walnut Loaf

This walnut olive loaf would have certainly pleased Elijah had the widow baked it for him. Unlike the widow, you may eventually run out of ingredients, but you'll never run out of the pleasure of eating it.

Non-stick vegetable oil cooking spray
1-1/2 cups all purpose flour, sifted
4 teaspoons double-acting baking powder
1 cup whole-wheat flour
1 egg, beaten
2 cups skim milk
1-1/2 tablespoons canola oil
1/2 cup walnuts, chopped
15 stuffed green olives, chopped

(1) Preheat oven to 375 degrees. Spray bread pan.
(2) Sift together all-purpose flour and baking powder. Mix in whole-wheat flour. In a separate bowl, whisk egg, milk and oil. Stir the mixtures together, just until moistened. Briefly mix in walnuts and chopped olives.
(3) Pour into baking pan. Bake 30 minutes, or until toothpick inserted in center of loaf comes out clean.

Servings: 8
Calories: 217
Fat (g.): 3.8
Sodium: 322 mg.

FIRE FROM HEAVEN

After Ahab died, his son Ahaziah became king. One day he fell from an upstairs room in his palace and was seriously hurt. The angel of the Lord told Elijah to meet the king's messengers and ask them, "Is it because there is no God in Israel that you have to go and ask Baal-zebub, the idol of the Philistines?" The Lord told Elijah that the king would die and Elijah told the messengers. The king was so angry that he sent fifty soldiers to capture Elijah and bring him to the king.

The men found Elijah sitting on the top of a hill. The men told him the king commanded him to come down. **Elijah said to the captain, "If I am a man of God, let fire come down from heaven and destroy you and your fifty men !" Then fire fell from heaven and killed them all.** *II Kings 1:10.*

The king sent fifty more men with another captain. **The captain said to him, "Man of God, the king says that you must come down right away."**

Elijah replied, "If I am a man of God, let fire come from heaven and destroy you and your fifty men!" And again the fire of God fell from heaven and killed them all. *II Kings 1: 11b-12.*

Once again the king sent a captain with fifty men. But this time the captain fell to his knees before Elijah. He pleaded with him, "O man of God, please spare my life and the lives of these, your fifty servants. See how the fire from heaven has destroyed the first two groups. But now please spare my life!"

Then the angel of the Lord said to Elijah, "Don't be afraid. Go with him." So Elijah got up and went to the king.

And Elijah said to the king, "This is what the Lord says: Why did you send messengers to Baal-zebub, the god of Ekron, as whether you will get well? Is there no God in Israel? Now, since you have done this, you will never leave the bed on which you are lying, but you will surely die."

So Ahaziah died, just as the Lord had promised through Elijah. *II Kings 13-17a.*

DID YOU KNOW?
King Ahaziah, as well as other evil kings in Israel and Judah, were guilty of "spiritual blindness." They refused to admit the sin in their lives. Those sins cost them their lives as well as others under their rule.

Fire From Heaven Chili

Elijah called fire from heaven upon his enemies, but you won't need to call fire from anywhere for this chili. Its tang of sweet fire will thrill your palate so much you won't even care about your enemies.

1 pound ground turkey (10% or less fat)
2 medium onions, chopped
2 green bell peppers, chopped
1 28-ounce pureed canned tomatoes
1 28-ounce can pinto beans
1 pkg. commercial chili seasoning
1 teaspoon garlic powder
1/2 teaspoon ground cumin
1/2 teaspoon crushed oregano
2 bottles of non-alcoholic beer

(1) Brown the ground turkey in a skillet.
(2) Meanwhile, in a Dutch oven, place onion, peppers, and tomatoes. Cook for 2-3 minutes. Add drained ground turkey, chili beans, seasonings, and beer. Bring to a boil and simmer, covered, for 50-60 minutes.

Suggestion: Serve over a bed of white or brown rice. Garnish with chopped onions, and grated fat-free cheese.

Servings: 4
Calories: 573
Fat (g.): 1.5
Sodium: 1238 mg.

A Chariot Ride to Heaven

When the Lord was about to take Elijah up to heaven in a whirlwind, Elijah and Elisha were traveling from Gilgal. And Elijah said to Elisha, "Stay here, for the Lord has told me to go to Bethel."

But Elisha replied, "As surely as the Lord lives and you yourself live, I will never leave you!" So they went on together to Bethel.

The group of prophets from Bethel came to Elisha and asked him, "Did you know that the Lord is going to take your master away from you today?"

"Quiet!" Elisha answered. "Of course I know it."

Then Elijah said to Elisha, "Stay here, for the Lord has told me to go to Jericho."

But Elisha replied again, "As surely as the Lord lives and you yourself live, I will never leave you." So they went on together to Jericho.

Then the group of prophets from Jericho came to Elisha and asked him, "Did you know that the Lord is going to take your master away from you today?"

"Quiet!" he answered again. "Of course I know it."

Then Elijah said to Elisha, "Stay here, for the Lord has told me to go to the Jordan River."

But again Elisha replied, "As surely as the Lord lives and you yourself live, I will never leave you." So they went on together.

Fifty men from the group of prophets also went and watched from a distance as Elijah and Elisha stopped beside the Jordan River. Then Elijah folded his cloak together and struck the water with it. The river divided, and the two of them went across on dry ground!

When they came to the other side, Elijah said to Elisha, "What can I do for you before I am taken away?"

And Elisha replied, "Please let me become your rightful successor."

"You have asked a difficult thing," Elijah replied. "If you see me when I am taken from you, then you will get your request. But if not, then you won't."

As they were walking along and talking, suddenly a chariot of fire appeared, drawn by horses of fire. It drove between them, separating them, and Elijah was carried by a whirlwind into heaven. Elisha saw it and cried out, "My father! My father! The chariots and charioteers of Israel!" As they disappeared from sight, Elisha tore his robe in two.

Then Elisha picked up Elijah's cloak and returned to the bank of the Jordan River. He struck the water with the cloak and cried out, "Where is the Lord, the God of Elijah?" Then the river divided, and Elisha went across.

When the group of prophets from Jericho saw what happened, they exclaimed, "Elisha has become Elijah's successor!" *II Kings 2:1-15a.*

DID YOU KNOW?

In the later ministry of Elijah, there are several important lessons to be learned: (1) it is fatal to forsake God, (2) it is necessary to honor his prophet, and (3) there is power and protection only in obedience to the God-given prophetic word.

Elisha's prophetic ministry was intended to show that there is no need, personal or national, that God cannot meet, all events are in His hands, and that He cares for His people.

Miracle Stuffed French Toast

This stuffed french toast is a miracle of taste that will make you think you're in heaven.

Non-stick vegetable oil cooking spray
1 loaf french bread, unsliced
1/2 cup egg substitute
1/3 cup skim milk
1 teaspoon vanilla
1 8-ounce pkg. fat-free cream cheese
1/3 cup orange marmalade
Powdered sugar
Fresh orange slices

(1) Spray large frying pan with cooking spray. Heat with medium heat until a drop or two of water sizzles.
(2) Meanwhile, mix egg substitute, milk, and vanilla together.
(3) Slice bread on a slight diagonal with a serrated knife and gently cut a slit pocket within 1/2 inch of each side of slice.
(4) Soften <u>unwrapped</u> cream cheese for 5 seconds in microwave. Mix with marmalade.
(5) Stuff 2 tablespoons of cream cheese mixture into pocket of bread slice. Close and secure with 1 or 2 toothpicks.
(6) Dip "pouch" quickly in egg mixture on both sides. Place in "sizzling" pan.
(7) Fry on each side about three minutes.

(8) Serve by placing on a individual plate. Sift powdered sugar lightly over toast and adorn with orange slices.

Note: May serve on a warm platter and let people help themselves.

Servings: 6 pouches
Calories: 282
Fat (g.): 2
Sodium: 216 mg.

THE PEOPLE REBUILD GOD'S TEMPLE

Samaritans were people who worshipped idols, yet pretended to serve God. They were angry and did all they could to stop the Jews by telling King Artaxerxes that they were disobeying him. He listened to them and he stopped the rebuilding of the Temple. After Artaxerxes' death, Darius I became king. The Jews didn't ask him for permission to start building the Temple again. Ever since the building of the Temple had stopped, the Samaritans built homes for themselves instead.

God was displeased with them and sent the prophet Haggai to tell them to build the Temple. Because they have built their own houses and not the Temple first, God had not blessed them nor prospered them. God was not happy.

The people obeyed the Lord's command and began to build the Temple. King Darius I commanded that the Temple be built without distraction.

When the builders completed the foundation of the Lord's Temple, the priests put on their robes and took their places to blow their trumpets. And the Levites, descendants of Asaph, clashed their cymbals to praise the Lord, just as King David had prescribed. With praise and thanks, they sang this song to the Lord:

> **"He is so good!**
> **His faithful love for Israel endures forever!"**

Then all the people gave a great shout, praising the Lord because the foundation of the Lord's Temple had been laid.

Many of the older priests, Levites, and other leaders remembered the first Temple, and they wept aloud when they saw the new Temple's foundation. The others, however, were shouting for joy. The joyful shouting and weeping mingled together in a loud commotion that could be heard far in the distance. *Ezra 3:10-13.*

DID YOU KNOW?

The people felt very, very happy. Their prayers and hopes were now being fulfilled before their very eyes. However, even with the completion of this Temple, it fell sadly short in grandeur to the one King Solomon had built for the Lord more than four hundred years earlier. That Temple had been destroyed.

Rebuilt Temple Club Sandwich

Just as the people rebuilt the Temple, stone upon stone, you can build this club sandwich, layer upon layer. An unusual and delightful touch is the addition of cranberry sauce with its deep royal hue, a treat to see as well as taste.

    16 slices thin-sliced low calorie white or wheat bread
    8 ounces deli-sliced white turkey
    6 tablespoons fat-free mayonnaise
    12 tablespoons whole berry cranberry sauce
    12 small lettuce leaves
    4 large black olives

<u>Assembly:</u>

(1) Toast bread. Spread each slice with 1/2 tablespoon of mayonnaise and 1 tablespoon of cranberry sauce. Place 3/4-ounce of turkey and one lettuce leaf on each slice.

(2) Stack one on top of the other and secure with <u>four</u> extra long toothpicks with olive inserted over them at top. Using serrated knife, cut through sandwich in an "X" fashion and place cut side up on individual serving place.

Suggestion: Delicious served with Spicy Oven Baked French Fries

Servings: 4
Calories: 270
Fat (g.): 2
Sodium: 856 mg.

FAITHFUL WORKERS REBUILD THE WALL

Ninety years had passed since the exiles had returned to Jerusalem from Babylon. Artaxerxes was the Persian king; Nehemiah, a Jew, was one of his trusted government officials. Some men from Judah told Nehemiah that the walls of Jerusalem were still in ruins, and the gates of the city had not been rebuilt. **When I (Nehemiah) heard this, I sat down and wept. In fact, for days I mourned, fasted, and prayed to the God of heaven. Then I said, "O Lord, God of heaven, the great and awesome God who keeps his covenant of unfailing love with those who love him and obey his commands, listen to my prayer! Look down and see me praying night and day for your people Israel. I confess that we have sinned against you. Yes, even my own family and I have sinned! We have sinned terribly by not obeying the commands, laws, and regulations that you gave us through your servant Moses."**

"Please remember what you told your servant Moses: 'If you sin, I will scatter you among the nations. But if you return to me and obey my commands, even if you are exiled to the ends of the earth, I will bring you back to the place I have chosen for my name to be honored.'"

"We are your servants, the people you rescued by your great power and might. O Lord, please hear my prayer! Listen to the prayers of those of us who delight in honoring you. Please grant me success now as I go to ask the king for a great favor. Put it into his heart to be kind to me." *Nehemiah 1:4-11.*

One day the king asked Nehemiah why he was so sad. Nehemiah prayed in his heart concerning this matter and then told him. The king let him go to Jerusalem.

Two wicked men, Sanballat and Tobiah, enemies of the Jews, tried to prevent the Jews from rebuilding the walls. **But when Sanballat, Tobiah, and Geshem the Arab heard of our plan, they scoffed contemptuously. "What are you doing, rebelling against the king like this?" they asked.**

But I replied, "The God of heaven will help us succeed. We his servants will start rebuilding this wall. But you have no stake or claim in Jerusalem." *Nehemiah 2:19,20.* Nehemiah reminded the Jews that the Lord would help them. There was much opposition. Nehemiah would not stop because he knew he was doing a great work. The people worked hard day and night to finish the wall. **So on October 2 the wall was finally finished -- just fifty-two days after we had begun. When our enemies and the surrounding nations heard about it, they were frightened and humiliated. They realized that this work had been done with the help of our God.** *Nehemiah 6:15,16.*

DID YOU KNOW?

When Nehemiah heard about the circumstances in Jerusalem, he immediately responded. Once he knew exactly what was needed, he was able to go to God in humble, honest prayer. He took responsibility for his part in the problem. He fully encountered his grief, then he was able to go on and ask and believe God would answer his prayer. He was empowered to do the work God had set before him to do.

Rebuilding The Wall Muffaletta

This is a sandwich for an army of wall-builders. Its sturdy size and healthful ingredients will make workers or picnickers happy in record time.

    1 jar (4-3/4 ounces) pimento-stuffed olives, drained and chopped
    1 large tomato, seeded and chopped
    1 rib celery, diced
    2 cloves garlic, minced
    1 tablespoon red wine vinegar
    1/2 teaspoon Italian seasoning
    1/4 teaspoon salt
    1/2 teaspoon freshly ground black pepper
    1 medium-size round Italian loaf of bread (about 9 inches in diameter, 1-1/4 pounds), cut in
      half horizontally
    1/4 pound each sliced low-fat pastrami, low-fat fat smoked turkey, fat-free swiss cheese,
      fat-free cheddar cheese

(1) Mix olives, tomato, celery, and garlic in bowl. Whisk vinegar, seasoning, salt, and pepper in another bowl. Add to olive mixture. Refrigerate at least 1 hour.

(2) Spoon 1 cup olive mixture over half of bread. Layer on meats and cheeses. Top with remaining olive mixture. Cover with bread top. Wrap loaf in plastic; place on baking sheet. Weight with heavy pot. Let stand at room temperature 1 hour. Cut in 8 wedges.

Servings: 8
Calories: 349
Fat (g.): 1.5
Sodium: 941 mg.

QUEEN ESTHER

King Xerxes loved Esther, a Jewess, and made her his queen.

There was an important man at the palace named Haman who had prevailed upon King Xerxes to sign into law a decree that all the Jews were to be killed by the people of Persia. This law horrified all the Jews, including Esther and her adopted father, Mordecai. Mordecai told her to go to the king and beg for their lives. There was a law that anyone going into the king without being asked by the king would be killed immediately.

Then Esther told Hathach to go back and relay this message to Mordecai: "The whole world knows that anyone who appears before the king in his inner court without being invited is doomed to die unless the king holds out his gold scepter. And the king has not called for me to come to him in more than a month." So Hattach gave Esther's message to Mordecai.

Mordecai sent back this reply to Esther: "Don't think for a moment that you will escape there in the palace when all other Jews are killed. If you keep quiet at a time like this, deliverance for the Jews will arise from some other place, but you and your relatives will die. What's more, who can say but that you have been elevated to the palace for such a time as this?"

Then Esther sent this reply to Mordecai: "Go and gather together all the Jews of Susa and fast for me. Do not eat or drink for three days, night or day. My maids and I will do the same. And, though it is against the law, I will go in to see the king. If I must die, I am willing to die." So Mordecai went away and did as Esther told him. *Esther 4:10-17.*

Esther did go into the king without being killed. While she was in with the king she invited him and Haman to a banquet. At the banquet the king asked Esther what he could give her. She asked the king to spare her life and the lives of all the Jews. She told the king that Haman wanted them killed. The king declared that Haman be hanged and made another law that the Jews could fight against anyone trying to harm them. They did, and destroyed all their enemies. They had a great celebration for their victory. **So on June 25 the king's secretaries were summoned. As Mordecai dictated, they wrote a decree to the Jews and to the princes, governors, and local officials of all the 127 provinces stretching from India to Ethiopia. The decree was written in the scripts and languages of all the peoples of the empire, including the Jews.** *Esther 8:9.*

The king's decree gave the Jews in every city authority to unite to defend their lives. They were allowed to kill, slaughter, and annihilate anyone of any nationality or province who might attack them or their children and wives, and to take the property of their enemies. The day chosen for this event throughout all the provinces of King Xerxes was March 7 of the next year. A copy of this decree was to be recognized as law in every

province and proclaimed to all the people. That way the Jews would be ready on that day to take revenge on their enemies. So urged on by the king's command, the messengers rode out swiftly on horses bred for the king's service. The same decree was also issued at the fortress of Susa.

Then Mordecai put on the royal robe of blue and white and the great crown of gold, and he wore an outer cloak of fine linen and purple. And the people of Susa celebrated the new decree. The Jews were filled with joy and gladness and were honored everywhere. In every city and province, wherever the king's decree arrived, the Jews rejoiced and had a great celebration and declared a public festival and holiday. And many of the people of the land became Jews themselves, for they feared what the Jews might do to them. *Esther 8:9,11-17.*

King Xerxes imposed tribute throughout his empire, even to the distant coastlands. His great achievements and the full account of the greatness of Mordecai, whom the king had promoted, are recorded in *The Book of the History of the Kings of Media and Persia.* Mordecai the Jew became the prime minister, with authority next to that of King Xerxes himself. He was very great among the Jews, who held him in high esteem, because he worked for the good of his people and was a friend at the royal court for all of them. *Esther 10:1-3.*

DID YOU KNOW?

Esther was desperately concerned for the fate of Israel as may be seen by the formula she used, which emphasized her personal relationship to the king. Not fully understanding the intricacies of Persian law, she appealed directly to the heart of the king for mercy upon Israel and for the reversal of "the letters devised by Haman," being careful not to put blame upon the king for his part in Haman's deed.

Anxious to show Esther that he did love her, the king began by reminding her of the favors he had already shown her. But he added that no one, not even the king of Persia himself, had the power to reverse the laws of the Medes and Persians. Nevertheless, Mordecai had the full right to issue a counter decree in the king's name, which would be just as irreversible as the one issued by Haman. This is what he did.

Queen Esther Vegetable Soup

The vegetables in this delicious soup are like the jewels of Esther's crown, but they cost less.

Non-stick olive oil cooking spray
3 large garlic cloves, minced
1-1/2 cups onion, chopped
1 cup uncooked barley
7 cups of vegetables (total): i.e., carrots, yellow crookneck squash, zucchini, patty pan
   squash, celery
8-9 cups water

1/4 cup cilantro, chopped
2-3 bay leaves
3 cups canned pureed tomatoes
1 teaspoon sugar
Salt and freshly ground pepper, to taste

(1) Spray a large Dutch oven with cooking spray and in it sauté garlic, onion, and barley, until onion is translucent.
(2) Stir in vegetables. Sauté 2 to 3 minutes.
(3) Add water. Bring to a boil. Add cilantro and bay leaves. Cover and reduce heat. Simmer about 40 minutes, or until vegetables and barley are just tender.
(4) Stir in tomatoes. Add sugar, salt, and pepper. Simmer 15 minutes longer, or until vegetables and barley are completely tender.
(5) Adjust seasonings. Discard bay leaves.

Serving: 8
Calories: 185
Fat (g.): .25
Sodium: 377 mg.

DEAD BONES BECOME A LIVING ARMY

The Lord showed Ezekiel a vision.

The Lord took hold of me, and I was carried away by the Spirit of the Lord to a valley filled with bones. He led me around among the old, dry bones that covered the valley floor. They were scattered everywhere across the ground. Then he asked me, "Son of man, can these bones become living people again?"

"O Sovereign Lord," I replied, "you alone know the answer to that."

Then he said to me, "Speak to these bones and say, 'Dry bones, listen to the word of the Lord! I am going to breathe into you and make you live again! I will put flesh and muscles on you and cover you with skin. I will put breath into you, and you will come to life. Then you will know that I am the Lord.'"

So I spoke these words, just as he told me. Suddenly as I spoke, there was a rattling noise all across the valley. The bones of each body came together and attached themselves as they had been before. Then as I watched, muscles and flesh formed over the bones. Then skin formed to cover their bodies, but they still had no breath in them.

Then he said to me, "Speak to the winds and say: 'This is what the Sovereign Lord says: Come, O breath, from the four winds! Breathe into these dead bodies so that they may live again.'"

So I spoke as he commanded me, and the wind entered the bodies, and they began to breathe. They all came to life and stood up on their feet -- a great army of them.

Then he said to me, "Son of man, these bones represent the people of Israel. They are saying, 'We have become old, dry bones - all hope is gone.' Now give them this message from the Sovereign Lord: O my people, I will open your graves of exile and cause you to rise again. Then I will bring you back to the land of Israel. When this happens, O my people, you will know that I am the Lord. I will put my Spirit in you, and you will live and return home to your own land. Then you will know that I am the Lord. You will see that I have done everything just as I promised. I, the Lord, have spoken!" *Ezekiel 37:1-13.*

DID YOU KNOW?

Even though the people continued to sin and God scattered them out in Canaan, Ezekiel told them the time would come when they would want to worship God, believe Him, accept Him as Savior, and obey Him.

Boney Biscuits

Here they are, row on row, biscuits arrayed like an army. They come to life in your mouth and their hot, spicy taste is a perfect complement to soups and salads.

Non-stick vegetable oil cooking spray
1-1/4 cups all-purpose flour
1/2 cup whole-wheat flour
1 tablespoon sugar
1-1/2 teaspoons baking powder
1 teaspoon baking soda
1/4 teaspoon salt
1 teaspoon chili powder
1 cup mashed potatoes
1 cup lowfat buttermilk
3 tablespoons "lite" butter, melted

(1) Preheat oven to 425 degrees.
(2) Combine first <u>seven</u> ingredients. Mix well and set aside.
(3) In a medium bowl, whisk together potatoes, buttermilk, and melted butter. Add buttermilk mixture to flour mixture and stir until a soft ball forms. Knead for one minute on a lightly floured surface (add more flour to dough, if needed, to prevent dough from sticking). Roll out 3/4-inch thick. Cut into 2-1/2-inch rounds using a cookie cutter.
(4) Spray cookie sheet. Transfer biscuits to cookie sheet. Bake 13-15 minutes, until biscuits are puffed up and golden brown.

Servings: 10
Calories: 135
Fat (g.): 2.9
Sodium: 89 mg

Three Men Who Walked in the Fire

King Nebuchadnezzar of Babylon made a huge statue of gold and set it on a plain in the province of Babylon and commanded the rulers of his kingdom to come and worship.

Daniel's three friends, Shadrach, Meshach, and Abednego, refused to do it because they knew it was wrong to worship a false god -- a statue. Some of the Babylonians went to the king and complained to him about them. They told the king that if they were thrown into the furnace, their God would save them. The king became furious and commanded that the three boys be bought to him. **Shadrach, Meshach, and Abednego replied, "O Nebuchadnezzar, we do not need to defend ourselves before you. If we are thrown into the blazing furnace, the God whom we serve is able to save us. He will rescue us from your power, Your Majesty. But even if he doesn't, Your Majesty can be sure that we will never serve your gods or worship the gold statue you have set up."** *Daniel 3:16-18.*

The king flew into a rage and ordered that the furnace be heated seven times hotter than it normally was. The three were thrown in and began to walk around in the flames. Nebuchadnezzar looked into the furnace and saw the three boys and a fourth, who looked like the Son of God. **Then Nebuchadnezzar came as close as he could to the door of the flaming furnace and shouted: "Shadrach, Meshach, and Abednego, servants of the Most High God, come out! Come here!" So Shadrach, Meshach, and Abednego stepped out of the fire. Then the princes, prefects, governors, and advisers crowded around them and saw that the fire had not touched them. Not a hair on their heads was singed, and their clothing was not scorched. They didn't even smell of smoke!**

Then Nebuchadnezzar said, "Praise to the God of Shadrach, Meshach, and Abednego! He sent his angel to rescue his servants who trusted in him. They defied the king's command and were willing to die rather than serve or worship any god except their own God. Therefore, I make this decree: If any people, whatever their race or nation or language, speak a word against the God of Shadrach, Meshach, and Abednego, they will be torn limb from limb, and their houses will be crushed into heaps of rubble. There is no other god who can rescue like this!" Then the king promoted Shadrach, Meshach, and Abednego to even higher positions in the province of Babylon. *Daniel 3:26-30.*

DID YOU KNOW?

If the three boys had not believed that God is sovereign, they might have decided that compromising on God's will was better than risking their own lives. If they had done that, they would not have experienced the wonderful victory that God gave to them. By handing it over to Him and following His will for them, they received great blessings.

Fiery Fajitas

These sizzling fajitas recall the heat of the furnace as they're brought to your table piping hot. This would have been a perfect dish for Shadrach, Meshach, and Abednego to celebrate their deliverance, and the King of Babylon would have liked them, too.

Non-stick vegetable oil cooking spray
3 tablespoons fresh lime juice
2 tablespoons chicken broth, defatted
1/2 teaspoon ground cumin
1/8 teaspoon ground red pepper
1/2 pound skinless, boneless chicken breasts, cut into thin strips
1/2 pound lean round steak, cut into thin strips
1 large sweet red pepper, cut into thin strips
1 large green pepper, cut into thin strips
1 large onion, thinly sliced
2 cups mushrooms, sliced
1-2 cloves garlic, minced
1/2 teaspoon freshly ground black pepper
12 medium fat-free flour tortillas, warmed
    Salsa, cilantro, fat-free cheese

(1) In a medium bowl, stir together the lime juice, broth, cumin, and ground red pepper. Add chicken and beef and toss until coated. Allow to marinate 30 minutes.
(2) Lightly spray an unheated large skillet. Heat over medium-high heat. Add the chicken/beef mixture; red and green peppers; onions, garlic, and black pepper. Cook and stir about 3 minutes or until chicken/beef mixture is no longer pink. Add mushrooms. Cook 30 seconds longer. Serve with tortillas and condiments.

Servings: 12
Calories: 217
Fat (g.): 3.2 (without condiments)
Sodium: 133 mg.

THE KING WHO ATE GRASS

King Nebuchadnezzar's palace was decorated with many beautiful objects and things stolen from nations he had conquered. He was a mighty king and his men flattered him by praising everything he did. He soon forgot about God and thought only of his own riches and power.

One night the king had a dream and he called for Daniel to interpret it.

"This is what the dream means, Your Majesty, and what the Most High has declared will happen to you. You will be driven from human society, and you will live in the fields with the wild animals. You will eat grass like a cow, and you will be drenched with the dew of heaven. Seven periods of time will pass while you live this way, until you learn that the Most High rules over the kingdoms of the world and gives them to anyone he chooses. But the stump and the roots were left in the ground. This means that you will receive your kingdom back again when you have learned that heaven rules."

"O King Nebuchadnezzar, please listen to me. Stop sinning and do what is right. Break from your wicked past by being merciful to the poor. Perhaps then you will continue to prosper."

"After this time had passed, I, Nebuchadnezzar, looked up to heaven. My sanity returned, and I praised and worshipped the Most High and honored the one who lives forever.

> **His rule is everlasting**
> > **and his kingdom is eternal.**
> **All the people of the earth are**
> > **nothing compared to him.**
> **He has the power to do as he pleases**
> > **among the angels of heaven**
> > **and with those who live on earth.**
> **No one can stop him or challenge him,**
> > **saying, 'What do you mean by doing**
> > > **these things?'"**

"When my sanity returned to me, so did my honor and glory and kingdom. My advisers and officers sought me out, and I was reestablished as head of my kingdom, with even greater honor than before.

"Now I, Nebuchadnezzar, praise and glorify and honor the King of heaven. All his acts are just and true, and he is able to humble those who are proud." *Daniel 4:34-37.*

DID YOU KNOW?

King Nebuchadnezzar saw that Daniel and his friends had more wisdom than any of his magicians or enchanters. This wisdom coming from God set them apart from other advisers and allowed them to triumph.

The King Who Ate Grass Coleslaw

For seven years King Nebuchadnezzar had to eat grass, and he certainly would have liked this coleslaw a lot better. It may be made only of fruits and vegetables, but this coleslaw would be honored even at a royal table.

1 pound green cabbage, finely shredded
2 large carrots, finely shredded
2 cups red cabbage, finely shredded
2 red apples, finely shredded
1-1/2 cups reduced-fat mayonnaise
1/2 cup reduced-fat sour cream
1/2 cup low-fat buttermilk
1/4 cup Dijon-style mustard
1/4 cup sugar
1 tablespoon celery seeds
1/2 teaspoon freshly ground black pepper

(1) Mix green and red cabbage, carrot, and apple in bowl.
(2) Whisk remaining ingredients in another bowl. Fold into cabbage mixture.
(3) Chill at least 3 hours.

Servings: 12
Calories: 67
Fat (g.): .4
Sodium: 211 mg

DANIEL IN THE LIONS' DEN

Darius the Mede decided to divide the kingdom into 120 provinces, and he appointed a prince to rule over each province. The king also chose Daniel and two others as administrators to supervise the princes and to watch out for the king' interests. Daniel soon proved himself more capable than all the other administrators and princes. Because of his great ability, the king made plans to place him over the entire empire. Then the other administrators and princes began searching for some fault in the way Daniel was handling his affairs, but they couldn't find anything to criticize. He was faithful and honest and always responsible. So they concluded, "Our only chance of finding grounds for accusing Daniel will be in connection with the requirements of his religion."

So the administrators and princes went to the king and said, "Long live King Darius! We administrators, prefects, princes, advisers, and other officials have unanimously agreed that Your Majesty should make a law that will be strictly enforced. Give orders that for the next thirty days anyone who prays to anyone, divine or human -- except to Your Majesty -- will be thrown to the lions. And let Your Majesty issue and sign this law so it cannot be changed, a law of the Medes and Persians, which cannot be revoked." So King Darius signed the law.

But when Daniel learned that the law had been signed, he went home and knelt down as usual in his upstairs room, with its windows open toward Jerusalem. He prayed three times a day, just as he had always done, giving thanks to his God. The officials went together to Daniel's house and found him praying and asking for God's help. So they went back to the king and reminded him about his law. The king agreed that he had signed that law.

So at last the king gave the order for Daniel to be arrested and thrown into the den of lions. The king said to him, "May your God, whom you worship continually, rescue you." A stone was brought and placed over the mouth of the den. The king sealed the stone with his own royal seal and the seals of his nobles, so that no one could rescue Daniel from the lions. Then the king returned to his palace and spent the night fasting. He refused his usual entertainment and couldn't sleep all that night.

Very early the next morning, the king hurried out to the lions' den. When he got there, he called out in anguish, "Daniel, servant of the living God! Was your God, whom you worship continually, able to rescue you from the lions?"

Daniel answered, "Long live the king! My God sent an angel to shut the lions' mouths so that they would not hurt me, for I have been found innocent in his sight. And I have not wronged you, Your Majesty."

The king was overjoyed and ordered that Daniel be lifted from the den. Not a scratch was found on him because he had trusted in his God. *Daniel 6:1-12,16-23.*

DID YOU KNOW?

Daniel was able to maintain spiritual vitality in the midst of a world that was hostile to his faith. The key to that vitality is regularly practicing spiritual disciplines: fasting, prayer, worship, Bible study, repentance, confession, and service.

Lions' Den Chicken Cacciatore Delight

If this dish had existed in Daniel's time, the king might have served it at the palace upon Daniel's release from the lions' den, for he valued him highly. What a way to celebrate!

4 boneless, skinless, chicken breasts, chopped into 1-inch pieces
1 large onion, chopped
4 garlic cloves, minced
4-1/2 cups defatted chicken broth
1 green bell pepper, cut into chunks
8 ounces mushrooms, sliced
1 10-ounce pkg. frozen peas, thawed
1/2 teaspoon dried oregano
1/2 teaspoon dried basil
1 bay leaf
26 ounces fat-free spaghetti sauce
2 cups rice, white or brown

(1) Pour a tablespoon of chicken broth into a Dutch oven. Heat on high, until the broth evaporates and browns. Add the chicken, onion, and garlic, letting it sit for a minute until it begins to brown. Add tiny amounts of broth to keep mixture from burning.
(2) Add bell pepper, oregano, basil, bay leaf, spaghetti sauce and 4 cups of chicken broth.
(3) Stir well and bring to a boil. Stir in rice, cover and reduce heat to low. Simmer 20 minutes for <u>white</u> rice, and 55 minutes for <u>brown</u> rice. Add peas, stir and serve.

Servings: 8
Calories: 252.5
Fat (g.): 2
Sodium: 1155 mg.

JONAH AND THE GREAT FISH

The Lord gave this message to Jonah son of Amittai: "Get up and go to the great city of Nineveh! Announce my judgment against it because I have seen how wicked its people are."

But Jonah got up and went in the opposite direction in order to get away from the Lord. He went down to the seacoast, to the port of Joppa, where he found a ship leaving for Tarshish. He bought a ticket and went on board, hoping that by going away to the west he could escape from the Lord.

But as the ship was sailing along, suddenly the Lord flung a powerful wind over the sea, causing a violent storm that threatened to send them to the bottom. Fearing for their lives, the desperate sailors shouted to their gods for help and threw the cargo overboard to lighten the ship. And all this time Jonah was sound asleep down in the hold. So the captain went down after him. "How can you sleep at a time like this?" he shouted. "Get up and pray to your god! Maybe he will have mercy on us and spare our lives."

Then the crew cast lots to see which of them had offended the gods and caused the terrible storm. When they did this, Jonah lost the toss. "What have you done to bring this awful storm down on us?" they demanded. "Who are you? What is your line of work? What country are you from? What is your nationality?"

And Jonah answered, "I am a Hebrew, and I worship the Lord, the God of heaven, who made the sea and the land." Then he told them that he was running away from the Lord. *Jonah 1:1-10a.* The men finally did what Jonah told them to do, which was to toss him into the sea. When they did, the storm stopped at once. **The sailors were awestruck by the Lord's great power, and they offered him a sacrifice and vowed to serve him.**

Now the Lord had arranged for a great fish to swallow Jonah. And Jonah was inside the fish for three days and three nights. *Jonah 1:16,17.*

Then Jonah prayed to the Lord his God from inside the fish. He said, "I cried out to the Lord in my great trouble, and he answered me. I called to you from the world of the dead, and the Lord, you heard me! You threw me into the ocean depth, and I sank down to the heart of the sea. I was buried beneath your wild and stormy waves. Then I said, 'O Lord, you have driven me from your presence. How will I ever again see your holy Temple?'"

"I sank beneath the waves, and death was very near. The waters closed in and around me, and seaweed wrapped itself around my head. I sank down to the very roots of the mountains. I was locked out of life and imprisoned in the land of the dead. But you, O Lord my God, have snatched me from the yawning jaws of death!"

"When I had lost all hope, I turned my thoughts once more to the Lord. And my earnest prayer went out to you in your holy Temple. Those who worship false gods turn their backs on all God's mercies. But I will offer sacrifices to you with songs of praise, and I will fulfill all my vows. For my salvation comes from the Lord alone."

Then the Lord ordered the fish to spit up Jonah on the beach, and it did.

Then the Lord spoke to Jonah a second time: "Get up and go to the great city of Nineveh, and deliver the message of judgment I have given you." *Jonah 2:1-3:1.*

This time Jonah obeyed the Lord's command and went to Nineveh, a city so large that it took three days to see it all.

DID YOU KNOW?

Jonah had finally obeyed the Lord by going to Nineveh and preaching God's message, but his heart attitude had not been changed to love. He so hated the Ninevites for their cruelty that deep in his heart he looked forward to their destruction.

The Ninevites were human beings -- men, women, and children -- objects of God's special creation, and, therefore, objects of His love. God's concern for man is unselfish. He seeks only to give comfort by delivering us from sin. No man has the right to question or resent the outpouring of God's love in saving man -- any man -- from sin and the destruction of sin. The Ninevites needed Jonah more than others because they had no one to show them moral distinctions.

Jonah's Spicy Salmon Loaf

You may never spend three days in the belly of a fish, but you'll be happy to fill your belly with this fish.

Non-stick vegetable oil cooking spray
2 14.75 ounce cans of pink salmon
1 large onion, chopped
2 large eggs
1/2 cup <u>seasoned</u> bread crumbs

(1) Preheat oven to 400 degrees.
(2) Spray loaf pan.
(3) Lightly mix together: salmon, onion, eggs, and bread crumbs.
(4) Place in pan and bake 40 minutes.
(5) Remove from oven, let rest 5 minutes, unmold onto serving platter.

Suggestion: A fun idea is to decorate the unmolded loaf with olive slices for eyes and mouth; yellow mustard squiggles for nose, fins, and scales.

Servings: 6
Calories 263
Fat (g.): 12
Sodium: 886 mg.

GOD'S SPECIAL MESSENGER

Here begins the Good News about Jesus the Messiah, the Son of God.

In the book of the prophet Isaiah, God said,

"Look , I am sending my messenger before you,
and he will prepare your way.
He is a voice shouting in the wilderness:
'Prepare a pathway for the Lord's coming!
Make a straight road for him!'"

This messenger was John the Baptist. He lived in the wilderness and was preaching that people should be baptized to show that they had turned from their sins and turned to God to be forgiven. People from Jerusalem and from all Judea traveled out into the wilderness to see and hear John. And when they confessed their sins, he baptized them in the Jordan River. His clothes were woven from camel hair, and he wore a leather belt; his food was locusts and wild honey. He announced: "Someone is coming soon who is far greater than I am -- so much greater than I am not even worthy to be his slave. I baptized you with water, but he will baptize you with the Holy Spirit!" *Mark 1:1-8.*

John can easily be overlooked as a significant spiritual leader of Israel because his primary ministry was to prepare the way for the Messiah, Jesus Christ. John's preparatory work for the coming of Jesus greatly helped the ministry of Jesus become immediately widespread. When it became clear that Jesus' ministry was overshadowing his own, John freely confessed, **"He must become greater and greater, and I must become less and less."** *John 3:30.*

DID YOU KNOW?
The nature of John the Baptist was full of impetuosity and fire -- a very Elijah. His life, however, was characterized by the graces of self-denial, humility, and holy courage.

Messenger Waffles with Buttery Maple Honey Syrup

John the Baptist lived on locusts and wild honey. We'll pass on the locusts, but pass that honey-flavored syrup for these unusual waffles.

Non-stick vegetable oil cooking spray
2 eggs
1 cup skim milk
1/2 cup molasses

1-1/2 tablespoons safflower or canola oil
1-1/2 cups all-purpose four
1/4 cup sugar
1 teaspoon ginger
1/2 teaspoon cloves
1 teaspoon cinnamon
1 teaspoon baking soda
2 teaspoons baking powder

Waffles:

(1) Plug in waffle iron.
(2) Beat eggs until light and fluffy. Add milk, molasses, and oil to eggs. Beat together.
(3) Sift together all dry ingredients into a large bowl. Stir egg mixture into dry mixture. Beat until smooth with a large whisk. Spray waffle iron when heated. Ladle batter onto waffle iron (amount varies with size of iron). Cook waffles on medium-high heat until light brown or desired crispness.

Note: Read directions on using iron, if applicable.

Syrup:

1 cup "lite" maple syrup
1/2 cup honey
2 tablespoons "lite" butter

(1) Cook syrup and honey for 10 minutes on medium-high heat. Add butter. Stir well until dissolved.

Waffles:
Servings: 4
Calories: 319
Fat (g.): 4.75
Sodium: 163 mg.

Syrup:
Servings: 4
Calories: 200
Fat (g.): 2
Sodium: 73 mg.

LET'S CELEBRATE JESUS' BIRTH

In the sixth month of Elizabeth's pregnancy, God sent the angel Gabriel to Nazareth, a village in Galilee, to a virgin named Mary. She was engaged to be married to a man named Joseph, a descendant of King David. Gabriel appeared to her and said, "Greetings, favored woman! The Lord is with you!"

Confused and disturbed, Mary tried to think what the angel could mean. "Don't be frightened, Mary," the angel told her, "for God has decided to bless you! You will become pregnant and have a son, and you are to name him Jesus. He will be very great and will be called the Son of the Most High. And the Lord God will give him the throne of his ancestor David. And he will reign over Israel forever; his Kingdom will never end!"

Mary asked the angel, "But how can I have a baby? I am a virgin."

The angel replied, "The Holy Spirit will come upon you, and the power of the Most High will overshadow you. So the baby born to you will be holy, and he will be called the Son of God. What's more, your relative Elizabeth has become pregnant in her old age! People used to say she was barren, but she's already in her sixth month. For nothing is impossible with God."

Mary responded, "I am the Lord's servant, and I am willing to accept whatever he wants. May everything you have said come true." And then the angel left. *Luke 1:26-38.*

At that time the Roman emperor, Augustus, decreed that a census should be taken throughout the Roman Empire. All returned to their own towns to register for this census. And because Joseph was a descendant of King David, he had to go to Bethlehem in Judea, David's ancient home. He traveled there from the village of Nazareth in Galilee. He took with him Mary, his fiancee, who was obviously pregnant by this time.

And while they were there, the time came for her baby to be born. She gave birth to her first child, a son. She wrapped him snugly in strips of cloth and laid him in a manger, because there was no room for them in the village inn.

That night some shepherds were in the fields outside the village, guarding their flocks of sheep. Suddenly, an angel of the Lord appeared among them, and the radiance of the Lord's glory surrounded them. They were terribly frightened, but the angel reassured them. "Don't be afraid!" he said. "I bring you good news of great joy for everyone! The Savior -- yes, the Messiah, the Lord -- has been born tonight in Bethlehem, the city of David! And this is how you will recognize him: You will find a baby lying in a manger, wrapped snugly in strips of cloth!"

Suddenly, the angel was joined by a vast host of others -- the armies of heaven -- praising God:

"Glory to God in the highest heaven,
   and peace on earth to all whom God favors." *Luke 2:1-14.*

DID YOU KNOW?

Although God is holy and mighty, the fact that Jesus came in the flesh gives us assurance that he is a personal God. God is with us and for us.

Celebration Cheesecake

Birthdays are usually celebrated with cakes, and this is a very special cheesecake for any occasion. What could be more special than the birth of Jesus Christ!

<u>Crust:</u>

1 prepared store-bought graham cracker crust (extra serving size)
2 tablespoons orange juice

(1) Preheat oven to 375 degrees. Sprinkle with orange juice on crust and bake 3 minutes, then chill.

<u>Filling:</u>

1/2 cup egg substitute or 2 egg whites
16 ounces <u>softened</u> non-fat cream cheese
1-1/2 cups non-fat sour cream
1 cup sugar
2 teaspoons vanilla extract
Pinch of salt

(1) Beat filling ingredients together. Pour into crust and bake about 55 minutes. Chill well before glazing.

<u>Topping Choices:</u>

Fresh fruit topping

1-1/2 cups fresh berries (such as blueberries, raspberries, boysenberries, and/or sliced strawberries)

(1) Place on cheesecake.

   OR

Cooked topping

1 cup blueberries <u>or</u>
1-1/2 cups strawberries <u>or</u>
1-1/2 cups raspberries <u>or</u>
1-1/2 cups boysenberries or blackberries

2 teaspoons quick tapioca
1 teaspoon lemon juice
1/2 cup sugar

(1) Combine one type of berries and tapioca in saucepan, crushing a few of them to release juice. Cook on low heat 5 minutes. Stir in lemon juice and sugar, then raise heat to moderate. Remove from heat and cool to room temperature before spreading on chilled cheesecake.

Servings: 10
Calories: 188
Fat (g.): 0
Sodium: 274 mg.

JESUS' BAPTISM

Then Jesus went from Galilee to the Jordan River to be baptized by John. But John didn't want to baptize him. "I am the one who needs to be baptized by you," he said, "so why are you coming to me?"

But Jesus said, "It must be done because we must do everything that is right." So then John baptized him.

After his baptism, as Jesus came up out of the water, the heavens were opened and he saw the Spirit of God descending like a dove and settling on him. And a voice from heaven said, "This is my beloved Son, and I am fully pleased with him." *Matt. 3:13-17.*

After Jesus was baptized, the Father commended his Son, Jesus, who was seen to be in perfect harmony with his Father and the Holy Spirit. The Holy Spirit appeared in the form of a dove.

DID YOU KNOW?

Jesus was baptized because it was the right thing to do and his actions modeled the importance of baptism to others.

Baptism Brownies

The baptism of Jesus certainly would have been a cause for celebration among all those who saw and heard about the event. Brownies are a delicious way to celebrate special events in our lives.

Non-stick vegetable oil cooking spray
1-3/4 cups sugar
3/4 cup unsweetened cocoa powder
1/2 cup all-purpose flour
1/2 cup whole-wheat flour
1/2 teaspoon baking powder
1-3/4 cups egg subsitute or 7 egg whites
2-4 ounce jars baby-food prunes
1/4 cup low-fat buttermilk
2 teaspoons vanilla
2/3 cup chopped walnuts
1 7-ounce jar marshmallow creme

(1) Preheat oven to 350 degrees. Lightly spray a 9" x 13" baking pan. Set pan aside.

(2) In a large bowl, stir together the sugar, cocoa, flour, whole wheat flour, and baking powder.

(3) In another large bowl, beat the egg whites until foamy. Slowly stir in the prunes, buttermilk, and vanilla. Add the egg mixture to the flour mixture and beat with an electric mixer until thoroughly combined. Fold in the walnuts.

(4) Transfer the batter to the prepared pan. Dot with tablespoons of marshmallow creme.

(5) Bake about 30 minutes or until the brownies just begin to pull away from the sides of the pan (<u>do not over bake</u>). Cool completely on a wire rack.

Servings: 36
Calories: 89
Fat (g): 2
Sodium: 111 mg.

THE MINISTRY OF JESUS

Jesus traveled throughout Galilee teaching in the synagogues, preaching everywhere the Good News about the Kingdom. And he healed people who had every kind of sickness and disease. News about him spread far beyond borders of Gailiee so that the sick were soon coming to be healed from as far away as Syria. And whatever their illness and pain, or if they were possessed by demons, or were epileptics, or were paralyzed -- he healed them all. Large crowds followed him wherever he went -- people from Galilee, the Ten Towns, Jerusalem, from all over Judea, and from east of the Jordan River. *Matthew 4:23-25.*

As Jesus was walking along, he saw a man who had been blind from birth. "Teacher," his disciples asked him, "why was this man born blind? Was it a result of his own sins or those of his parents?"

"It was not because of his sins or his parents' sins," Jesus answered. "He was born blind so the power of God could be seen in him. All of us must quickly carry out the tasks assigned us by the one who sent me, because there is little time left before the night falls and all work comes to an end. But while I am still here in the world, I am the light of the world."

Then he spit on the ground, made mud with the saliva, and smoothed the mud over the blind man's eyes. He told him, "Go and wash in the pool of Siloam." So the man went and washed, and came back seeing! *John 9:1-7.*

Some of the Pharisees tried to talk the man out of the miracle he received. The man refused to comply with them. The Pharisees finally threw him out of the synagogue.

When Jesus heard what had happened, he found the man and said, "Do you believe in the Son of Man?"

The man answered, "Who is he, sir, because I would like to see him."

"You have seen him," Jesus said, "and he is speaking to you!"

"Yes, Lord," the man said, "I believe!" And he worshipped Jesus. *John 9:35-38.*

DID YOU KNOW?

When we recognize that Jesus is our deliverer and our healer, we begin to gain our spiritual sight.

Bright Eyes Carrots

Let not your eyes grow dim so that you fail to see the "Light of the World." Maintain your physical eyesight with this savory carrot dish.

    1 small bag of baby carrots
    1 teaspoon <u>each</u> grated orange and lemon zest
    1 tablespoon low-fat butter
    1 teaspoon dill weed

(1) Steam or boil carrots until tender, about 15 minutes.
(2) Remove from heat. Place in serving bowl. Gently toss with butter and sprinkle with dill weed and citrus zests.

Servings: 4
Calories: 95
Fat (g.): 2
Sodium: 43 mg.

THE SERMON ON THE MOUNT

One day as the crowds were gathering, Jesus went up the mountainside with his disciples and sat down to teach them.

This is what he taught them:

"God blesses those who realize their need for him,
   for the Kingdom of Heaven is given to them.
God blesses those who mourn,
   for they will be comforted.
God blesses those who are gentle and lowly,
   for the whole earth will belong to them.
God blesses those who are hungry and thirsty for justice,
   for they will receive it in full.
God blesses those who are merciful,
   for they will be shown mercy.
God blesses those whose hearts are pure,
   for they will see God.
God blesses those who work for peace,
   for they will be called the children of God.
God blesses those who are persecuted because they live for God,
   for the Kingdom of Heaven is theirs."

"God blesses you when you are mocked and persecuted and lied about because you are my followers. Be happy about it! Be very glad! For a great reward awaits you in heaven. And remember, the ancient prophets were persecuted, too." *Matthew 5:1-11.*

True spiritual renewal comes first by the way of humility. The cure begins when we accept our personal problems and failures. Sometimes, we have to grieve and mourn over our failures and losses. This way, God is able to comfort us as only He can. This is a key step in spiritual growth.

DID YOU KNOW?
Persecution is likely to come to us as we are trying to live by God's principles. It is always more important to please God than man. As we do things God's way according to the teachings of the Bible, we are able to build healthy relationships with God and others.

Beatitudes Breakfast Casserole

Starting the day off right with the Bible and prayer, a willing heart, and a good breakfast will give you the strength to follow the Beatitudes.

1 large loaf french bread, crusts removed and diced
1 large onion, chopped
6 ounces fat-free cheddar cheese
4 ounces fat-free swiss cheese
2-1/2 cups skim milk
2-1/2 cups egg substitute or 10 egg whites
1/2 pound very low-fat turkey bacon
1 pkg. mushrooms, sliced
1 large green or red bell pepper, diced

(1) Preheat oven to 350 degrees.
(2) Melt cheese and <u>one</u> cup of milk together over medium-low heat. Mix the remaining milk with egg whites.
(3) Spray 9" x 13" pan and place bread, bacon, and onion in it. Pour cheese mixture over bread cubes and onions. Pour egg mixture on top. Sprinkle with mushrooms and bell pepper. Cover with aluminum foil and refrigerate overnight.
(4) Bake for one hour <u>covered with foil</u> or until middle is set.

Servings: 10
Calories: 192
Fat (g.): 2
Sodium: 331 mg.

JESUS CHOOSES TWELVE APOSTLES

Afterward Jesus went up on a mountain and called the ones he wanted to go with him. And they came to him. Then he selected twelve of them to be his regular companions, calling them apostles. He sent them out to preach, and he gave them authority to cast out demons. These are the names of the twelve he chose:

Simon (he renamed him Peter),
James and John (the sons of Zebedee, but Jesus nicknamed them "Sons of Thunder"),
Andrew,
Philip,
Bartholomew,
Matthew,
Thomas,
James (son of Alphaeus),
Thaddaeus,
Simon (the Zealot),
Judas Iscariot (who later betrayed him). *Mark 3:13-19.*

DID YOU KNOW?

The purpose of Jesus appointing twelve apostles was twofold: (1) that they should be with Him for companionship and training, and (2) that they might go out to preach and cast out demons.

Chocolate Cherry Torte For Twelve

With his team of twelve in place, Jesus was ready to begin his ministry. You can reward your team, large or small, for their work by serving them a large piece of chocolate cherry torte.

Non-stick vegetable oil cooking spray
Flour
1 pkg. chocolate cake mix
3/4 cup egg substitute or 3 egg whites
1 cup water
1/3 cup applesauce
2 jars fat-free hot fudge sauce
2 21-ounce cans cherry pie filling
1 can fat-free whipped topping (preferably aerosol can)
6-8 whole pecans or walnut halves

(1) Spray <u>two</u> 8-inch cake pans with spray and dust with flour. Prepare cake mix according to package directions, using egg substitute, water, and applesauce. Bake according to package directions. Cool completely on wire rack.

(2) Place one layer on clear glass plate, preferably footed.* Pour one jar of fudge sauce over bottom layer until it's within 1-inch of edge. Carefully smooth out evenly with spatula. Carefully spoon cherry filling over fudge sauce. Leave most of the "sauce" in the can. Place second layer on top. Repeat with fudge sauce and cherries. Decorate with whipped cream in small "clouds" around base of torte and on top. Place a nut in center of each "cloud" on the top of the torte.

(3) Refrigerate one hour before serving, or decorate just before serving.

*A footed cake plate makes for a better presentation, but is not required.

Serving: 12
Calories: 418
Fat (g.): 4.5
Sodium: 432 mg.

JESUS TURNS WATER INTO WINE

The next day Jesus' mother was a guest at a wedding celebration in the village of Cana in Galilee. Jesus and his disciples were also invited to the celebration. The wine supply ran out during the festivities, so Jesus' mother spoke to him about the problem. "They have no more wine," she told him.

"How does that concern you and me?" Jesus asked. "My time has not yet come."

But his mother told the servants, "Do whatever he tells you."

Six stone waterpots were standing there; they were used for Jewish ceremonial purposes and held twenty to thirty gallons each. Jesus told the servants, "Fill the jars with water." When the jars had been filled to the brim, he said, "Dip some out and take it to the master of ceremonies." So they followed his instructions.

When the master of ceremonies tasted the water that was now wine, not knowing where it had come from (though, of course, the servants knew), he called the bridegroom over. "Usually a host serves the best wine first," he said. "Then, when everyone is full and doesn't care, he brings out the less expensive wines. But you have kept the best until now!" *John 2:1-10.*

DID YOU KNOW?
Jesus's mother, Mary, came to him with the need for more wine for the wedding guests. She may have wanted Jesus to do a miracle in front of others that would draw attention to himself. He refused, his hour had not come. Jesus said, "What have I to do with thee?" Jesus wanted his mother to understand that the former relationship of him submitting to his mother was at an end. Since she could not command him any longer, she could instruct the servants to obey his directions. She did.

Miracle Berry Punch

You may never want to serve six stone waterpots of wine, but you'll love to serve and drink this berry punch.

    1 liter bottle of diet lemon lime soda
    1 64-ounce bottle of cranberry raspberry juice cocktail
      Lemon slices

(1) Mix together. Pour over ice in a tall clear glass or place in a punch bowl with a large ring of ice floating on the surface or just lots of ice cubes and slices of lemon in the bowl.

Servings: 12
Calories: 110
Fat (g.): 0
Sodium: 18 mg.

TWO BOATS FILLED WITH FISH

One day as Jesus was preaching on the shore of the Sea of Galilee, great crowds pressed in on him to listen to the word of God. He noticed two empty boats at the water's edge, for the fisherman had left them and were washing their nets. Stepping into one of the boats, Jesus asked Simon, its owner, to push it out into the water. So he sat in the boat and taught the crowds from there.

When he had finished speaking, he said to Simon, "Now go out where it is deeper and let down your nets, and you will catch many fish."

"Master," Simon replied, "We worked hard all last night and didn't catch a thing. But if you say so, we'll try again." And this time their nets were so full they began to tear! A shout for help brought their partners in the other boat, and soon both boats were filled with fish and on the verge of sinking.

When Simon Peter realized what had happened, he fell to his knees before Jesus and said, "Oh, Lord, please leave me -- I'm too much of a sinner to be around you." For he was awestruck by the size of their catch, as were the others with him. His partners, James and John, the sons of Zebedee, were also amazed.

Jesus replied to Simon, "Don't be afraid! From now on you'll be fishing for people!" And as soon as they landed, they left everything and followed Jesus. *Luke 5:1-11.*

DID YOU KNOW?
Peter was a skilled fisherman. Even though he was quite sure that they would catch nothing when Jesus told him to let down his nets, by doing so, Peter showed faith in Jesus. He was ready to believe the Master's word even in matters in which Jesus would not be naturally considered an expert.

Clam Chowder & Seafood Chowder in Two Boats

These two chowder recipes could be multiplied for large groups to commemorate the miraculous catches of fish by some of the apostles. Let down your nets and enjoy your fill.

Clam Chowder:

2 6-1/2 ounce cans minced clams (with juice)
2-1/2 cups potatoes, peeled and finely chopped
1 cup onions, chopped

1 teaspoon instant chicken bouillon granules
1 teaspoon Worcestershire sauce
1/4 teaspoon diced thyme
1/8 teaspoon freshly ground pepper
1-1/2 cups 1% milk
3 tablespoons cornstarch
1-1/2 cups evaporated skim milk
1/4 teaspoon liquid smoke
1-1/2 cups frozen corn

(1) Drain the clams, reserving the juices. Add enough water to make 1 cup clam juice, if needed.
(2) In a medium saucepan, combine juice mixture, potatoes, onions, bouillon granules, Worcestershire sauce, thyme, and black pepper. Bring to a boil, then reduce the heat. Cover and simmer about 5 minutes or until the potatoes are tender. Using the back of a fork, mash some of the potatoes against the side of the saucepan.
(3) In a small bowl, stir together the 1% milk and cornstarch. Add the cornstarch mixture, evaporated skim milk and liquid smoke to the potato mixture. Cook and stir until slightly thickened and bubbly. Stir in the clams. Return to a boil, then reduce heat. Add corn. Cook for 1 minute, stirring frequently.

Seafood Chowder:

Non-stick vegetable oil cooking spray
1 cup onions, chopped
1 cup mushrooms, sliced
2 garlic cloves, minced
2 6-1/2 ounce cans shucked clams and their juice
2 cups low-sodium, reduced-fat chicken broth
1/2 cup non-alcoholic wine
1-1/2 cups peeled, cubed potatoes
1/2 cup celery, chopped
1/2 cup carrots, chopped
1/4 cup green onion, chopped
1/2-pound fish fillets (i.e. red snapper, cod, haddock) cut in chunks
3/4 teaspoon dried basil
1 teaspoon "lite" Worcestershire sauce
3-4 drops hot pepper sauce
1/2 teaspoon salt
1/2 teaspoon freshly ground pepper
2 tablespoons fresh parsley, chopped
1/3 cup evaporated skim milk
3/4 cup fat-free sour cream

(1) Spray a large saucepan. Add onions, mushrooms, and garlic. Cook over medium heat until vegetables are softened, about 5 minutes.
(2) Meanwhile, drain and reserve juice of clams. Set clams aside. Add reserved clam juice to onions and mushrooms, along with chicken broth, wine, potatoes, celery, carrots, and green

onions. Bring to a boil. Reduce heat to medium. Cover and cook for 15 minutes, until potatoes are tender.

(3) Add clams, fish chunks, basil, Worcestershire sauce, hot pepper sauce, salt, and pepper. Simmer over medium heat for 5 minutes, until fish turns opaque.

(4) Turn heat low. Gradually stir in evaporated skim milk, then sour cream. Add parsley and continue to stir until heated through. <u>DO NOT BOIL.</u>

Clam Chowder:
Servings: 4 main servings
Calories: 246
Fat (g.): 1
Sodium: 235 mg.

Seafood Chowder:
Servings: 4 main servings
Calories: 290
Fat (g.): .5
Sodium: 175 mg.

MIRACLE AT THE PICNIC

Jesus returned to the Sea of Galilee and climbed a hill and sat down. A vast crowd brought him the lame, blind, crippled, mute, and many others with physical difficulties, and they laid them before Jesus. And he healed them all. The crowd was amazed! Those who hadn't been able to speak were talking, the crippled were made well, the lame were walking around, and those who had been blind could see again! And they praised the God of Israel.

Then Jesus called his disciples to him and said, "I feel sorry for these people. They have been here with me for three days, and they have nothing left to eat. I don't want to send them away hungry, or they will faint along the road."

The disciples replied, "And where would we get enough food out here in the wilderness for all of them to eat?"

Jesus asked, "How many loaves of bread do you have?"

They replied, "Seven, and a few small fish." So Jesus told all the people to sit down on the ground. Then he took the seven loaves and the fish, thanked God for them, broke them into pieces, and gave them to the disciples, who distributed the food to the crowd.

They all ate until they were full, and when the scraps were picked up, there were seven large baskets of food left over! There were four thousand men who were fed that day, in addition to all the women and children. Then Jesus sent the people home, and he got into a boat and crossed over to the region of Magadan. *Matthew 15:29-39.*

DID YOU KNOW?
Jesus is a miracle worker.

Tuna Picnic Sandwich

The bread and the fish go together in this scrumptious sandwich which reminds us of the miracle of the loaves and fishes. However, I can't promise you'll have any leftovers.

4 tuna steaks, about 6 inches each and 1-inch thick
2 tablespoons <u>each</u> of lime juice, cilantro, reduced sodium soy sauce, honey,
    tomato-based chili sauce
2 teaspoons olive oil
Shredded lettuce

Sliced tomato
Fat-free mayonnaise
4 large rolls, preferably poppy seed or kaiser

(1) Rinse tuna steaks and pat dry. Arrange tuna in a 9" x 13" glass baking dish. Mix lime, cilantro, soy sauce, honey, chili sauce and olive oil in a small bowl. Pour over tuna. Turn fish to coat with marinade. Cover and refrigerate for 1-2 hours.
(2) Prepare grill (medium-high setting). Remove tuna from marinade. Discard marinade. Cook tuna over hot coals for 4-5 minutes on each side. Fish should be lightly browned on outside and pale pink in thickest part. Remove from heat.
(3) Serve on a large, fresh roll garnished with mayonnaise, lettuce, and tomato.

Servings: 4
Calories: 367
Fat (g.): 0
Sodium: 650 mg.

THE GOOD SAMARITAN

One day an expert in religious law stood up to test Jesus by asking him this question: "Teacher, what must I do to receive eternal life?"

Jesus replied, "What does the law of Moses say? How do you read it?"

The man answered, "'You must love the Lord your God with all your heart, all your soul, all your strength, and all your mind.' And, 'Love your neighbor as yourself.'"

"Right!" Jesus told him. "Do this and you will live!"

The man wanted to justify his actions, so he asked Jesus, "And who is my neighbor?"

Jesus replied with an illustration: "A Jewish man was traveling on a trip from Jerusalem to Jericho, and he was attacked by bandits. They stripped him of his clothes and money, beat him up, and left him half dead beside the road."

"By chance a Jewish priest came along; but when he saw the man lying there, he crossed to the other side of the road and passed him by. A Temple assistant walked over and looked at him lying there, but he also passed by on the other side."

"Then a despised Samaritan came along, and when he saw the man, he felt deep pity. Kneeling beside him, the Samaritan soothed his wounds with medicine and bandaged them. Then he put the man on his own donkey and took him to an inn, where he took care of him. The next day he handed the innkeeper two pieces of silver and told him to take care of the man. 'If his bill runs higher than that,' he said, 'I'll pay the difference the next time I am here.'"

"Now which of these three would you say was a neighbor to the man who was attacked by bandits?" Jesus asked.

The man replied, "The one who showed him mercy."

Then Jesus said, "Yes, now go and do the same." *Luke 10:25-37.*

DID YOU KNOW?

Jesus showed in this parable that the Samaritan had the attitude of love which the Law commanded. If the robbers who had hurt the man were still in the vicinity, the Samaritan was risking his life to help the man.

Good Samaritan Tabbouleh

Tabbouleh is a traditional Middle Eastern dish. Something like it may very well have been served by people at the inn who cared for the wounded man. Be a Good Samaritan to your friends and family by serving them this tasty salad.

Salad:

3/4 cup bulgar
3/4 cups boiling water
2 tomatoes, chopped
1/2 cup zucchini, finely diced
3/4 cup snipped fresh parsley
1/4 cup snipped fresh chives
1/4 cup snipped fresh mint

To make the salad:
(1) In a large bowl, stir together bulgar and water. Let stand about 15 minutes or until water is absorbed. Gently stir in the tomatoes, zucchini, parsley, chives, and mint. Set aside.

Dressing:

1/4 cup fresh lemon juice
2 tablespoons canned chicken broth, defatted
1 tablespoon olive oil
1 clove garlic, minced

To make the dressing:
(1) Stir the above ingredients together and add to the bulgar mixture. Gently stir until combined. Cover and chill in the refrigerator for at least 2 hours to blend the flavors.

Servings: 8 side-dish serving
Calories: 211
Fat (g.): 1.5
Sodium: 5 mg.

JESUS LOVES CHILDREN

Some children were brought to Jesus so he could lay his hands on them and pray for them. The disciples told them not to bother him. But Jesus said, "Let the children come to me. Don't stop them! For the Kingdom of Heaven belongs to such as these." And he put his hands on their heads and blessed them before he left. *Matt. 19:13-15.*

DID YOU KNOW?
Jesus was always interested in the young and the weak. Since entrance into His Kingdom requires that men become childlike in faith, Jesus wants not only the disciples but all of us to be more gracious to actual children.

Children of the World Cookies

These cookies, which can be colored to represent all the races of the world, help us remember all the races of the world and that Jesus loves us all equally.

Cookie Dough:

      1 box fluffy white frosting mix
      1 cup powdered sugar
      2 teaspoons vanilla extract
      1 teaspoon lemon extract
      1/4 cup evaporated skim milk
      1/2 cup egg substitute or 2 egg whites
      4 tablespoons "lite" butter
      3 cups self-rising flour
          Flour

(1) Preheat oven to 375 degrees.
(2) Cream together frosting mix, powdered sugar, butter, lemon, vanilla, and skim milk with an electric mixer. Add 1/2 cup egg substitute and continue to blend. Stir in 3 cups self-rising flour.
(3) Place the dough in the refrigerator for 30 minutes.
(4) Roll the dough out on a floured surface and cut into the desired shapes.
(5) Place on a cookie sheet that has been sprayed with cooking spray.
(6) Bake 7-8 minutes or until golden brown. Cool on a wire rack. Frost with cream cheese frosting.

Additions:

For brown or dark brown children, add cocoa.
For yellow children, add drops of yellow food coloring.
For red children, add drops of red food coloring.

Frosting:

4 tablespoons "lite" butter
2 tablespoons fat-free cream cheese
2-1/2 to 3 cups powdered sugar, sifted
1 teaspoon vanilla
1/4 teaspoon lemon extract
1-2 teaspoons skim milk

(1) Blend together all of the above ingredients with an electric mixer until smooth and creamy.
(2) Place in the refrigerator 20-30 minutes. Frosting will harden slightly.

Cookies:
Servings: 12
Calories: 205
Fat (g.): 2.7
Sodium: 487 mg.

Frosting:
Servings: 12
Calories: 125
Fat (g.): 2.7
Sodium: 35 mg.

Jesus' Triumphal Entry

As Jesus and his disciples approached Jerusalem, they came to the towns of Bethphage and Bethany, on the Mount of Olives. Jesus sent two of them on ahead. "Go into that village there," he told them, "and as soon as you enter it, you will see a colt tied there that has never been ridden. Untie it and bring it here. If anyone asked what you are doing, just say, 'The Lord needs it and will return it soon.'"

The two disciples left and found the colt standing in the street, tied outside a house. As they were untying it, some bystanders demanded, "What are you doing, untying that colt?" They said what Jesus had told them to say, and they were permitted to take it. Then they brought the colt to Jesus and threw their garments over it, and he sat on it.

Many in the crowd spread their coats on the road ahead of Jesus, and others cut leafy branches in the fields and spread them along the way. He was in the center of the procession, and the crowds all around him were shouting.

"Praise God!
　　Bless the one who comes in the name of the Lord!
Bless the coming kingdom of our ancestor David!
　　Praise God in highest heaven!"

So Jesus came to Jerusalem and went into the Temple. He looked around carefully at everything, and then he left because it was late in the afternoon. Then he went out to Bethany with the twelve disciples. *Mark 11:1-11.*

DID YOU KNOW?
Some theologians believe the triumphal entry of Jesus into Jerusalem should not be viewed in the light of a glorious King, but as a Savior who was soon to suffer.

Hearts of Palm Salad with Vinaigrette Dressing

Palm fronds are traditionally thought to be the branches that the people threw into the path of Jesus' donkey, and his triumphal entry is still celebrated today throughout the Christian world as Palm Sunday. This hearts of palm salad, therefore, is a reminder of that remarkable day!

Salad:

1 bunch red leaf lettuce, washed and torn into bite-size pieces
1 15-ounce can hearts of palm

Vinaigrette Dressing:

1 small onion, finely chopped
2 tablespoons cider vinegar
2 tablespoons canola oil
    Salt and freshly ground pepper, to taste
    Tomato wedges

(1) Chill can of hearts of palm and serving plates.
(2) Mix together all ingredients, except hearts of palm and lettuce.
(3) At serving time, place lettuce on plates. Place hearts of palm equally on plates, if possible. Place tomato wedges alongside "hearts." Spoon vinaigrette over salad and serve.

Servings: 4
Calories: 81
Fat (g.): 3.5
Sodium: 138 mg.

THE DEATH, BURIAL, AND RESURRECTION OF JESUS

So they took Jesus and led him away. Carrying the cross by himself, Jesus went to the place called Skull Hill. There they crucified him. There were two others crucified with him, one on either side, with Jesus between them. And Pilate posted a sign over him that read, "Jesus of Nazareth, the King of the Jews." The place where Jesus was crucified was near the city; and the sign was written in Hebrew, Latin, and Greek, so that many people could read it.

Then the leading priests said to Pilate, "Change it from 'The King of the Jews' to 'He said, I am King of the Jews.'"

Pilate replied, "What I have written, I have written. It stays exactly as it is."

When the soldiers had crucified Jesus, they divided his clothes among the four of them. They also took his robe, but it was seamless, woven in one piece from the top. So they said, "Let's not tear it but throw dice to see who gets it." This fulfilled the Scripture that says, "They divided my clothes among themselves and threw dice for my robe." So that is what they did.

Standing near the cross were Jesus' mother, and his mother's sister, Mary, and Mary Magdalene. When Jesus saw his mother standing there beside the disciple he loved, he said to her, "Woman, he is your son." And he said to this disciple, "She is your mother." And from then on this disciple took her into his home.

Jesus knew that everything was now finished, and to fulfill the Scripture he said, "I am thirsty." A jar of sour wine was sitting there, so they soaked a sponge in it, put it on a hyssop branch, and held it up to his lips. When Jesus had tasted it, he said, "It is finished!" Then he bowed his head and gave up his spirit. *John 19:16b-30.*

Joseph of Arimathea and Nicodemus **together wrapped Jesus' body in a long linen cloth with the spices, as is the Jewish custom of burial. The place of crucifixion was near a garden, where there was a new tomb, never used before. And so, because it was the day of preparation before the Passover and since the tomb was close at hand, they laid Jesus there.**

Early Sunday morning, while it was still dark, Mary Magdalene came to the tomb and found that the stone had been rolled away from the entrance. She ran and found Simon Peter and the other disciple, the one whom Jesus loved. She said, "They have taken the Lord's body out of the tomb, and I don't know where they have put him!"

Peter and the other disciple ran to the tomb to see. The other disciple outran Peter and got there first. He stooped and looked in and saw the linen cloth lying there, but he didn't go in. Then Simon Peter arrived and went inside. He also noticed the linen wrappings lying there, while the cloth that had covered Jesus' head was folded up and lying to the side. Then the other disciple also went in, and he saw and believed -- for until then they hadn't realized that the Scriptures said he would rise from the dead. Then they went home. *John 19:40-42; 20:1-10.*

DID YOU KNOW?

Confession with the mouth and belief in the heart refer to the believer's outward and inward responses. His inward conviction must find outward expression. When he confesses that Jesus is Lord, he is asserting Christ's deity and his exaltation, and the fact that he, the believer, belongs to Him. A man's belief in the Resurrection shows that he knows God acted and triumphed in the cross. The man who confesses that Christ is Lord and has such a belief or conviction will attain salvation.

Resurrection Sundae

This magnificent sundae with its emphasis on the colors white and gold can remind us of the most glorious event in human history.

1 quart fat-free vanilla or butterscotch ripple ice cream
1 cup caramel butterscotch low-fat fudge sauce
4 cups fat-free whipped cream, preferably from an aerosol can
4 tablespoons pecans, chopped
8 "rolled" Italian cookies

(1) In a sundae dish, place one large scoop of ice cream. Place fudge sauce on top of ice cream. From an aerosol can, squeeze about a cup of whipped cream. Drizzle over cream a little fudge sauce. Sprinkle with nuts and place 2 cookies into whipped cream.

Servings: 4
Calories: 721
Fat (g.): 5.75
Sodium: 245 mg.

THE GOOD NEWS IS FOR EVERYONE

Then Peter replied, "I see very clearly that God doesn't show partiality. In every nation he accepts those who fear him and do what is right. I'm sure you have heard about the Good News for the people of Israel -- that there is peace with God through Jesus Christ, who is Lord of all. You know what happened all through Judea, beginning in Galilee after John the Baptist began preaching. And no doubt you know that God anointed Jesus of Nazareth with the Holy Spirit and with power. Then Jesus went around doing good and healing all who were oppressed by the devil, for God was with him."

"And we apostles are witnesses of all he did throughout Israel and in Jerusalem. They put him to death by crucifying him, but God raised him to life three days later. Then God allowed him to appear, not to the general public, but to us whom God had chosen beforehand to be his witnesses. We were those who ate and drank with him after he rose from the dead. And he ordered us to preach everywhere and to testify that Jesus is ordained of God to be the judge of all -- the living and the dead. He is the one all the prophets testified about, saying that everyone who believes in him will have their sins forgiven through his name."

Even as Peter was saying these things, the Holy Spirit fell upon all who had heard the message. The Jewish believers who came with Peter were amazed that the gift of the Holy Spirit had been poured out upon the Gentiles, too. And there could be no doubt about it, for they heard them speaking in tongues and praising God. *Acts 10:34-46.*

DID YOU KNOW?

On the day of Pentecost, the disciples waited in Jerusalem just as Jesus had told them to do. Suddenly the Holy Spirit manifested his presence by sound (wind), sight (fire), and speech (new language). The believers were filled with the Holy Spirit, and God's renewing power began its work of transforming them from the inside out. This marked a new era in history as God's powerful presence entered the lives of all believers.

Pentecost Pancakes

You'll feel like speaking in tongues after you've eaten these fluffy potato pancakes -- light and crisp. The humble potato can be made into this tasty dish, just as the Good News is for everyone.

Non-stick vegetable oil cooking spray
2 cups coarsely grated large potatoes <u>or</u> 4 cups frozen grated potatoes, thawed and drained
2 eggs
1/2 cup egg substitute or 2 egg whites
1-1/2 tablespoons flour
1 teaspoon salt
2 tablespoons onion, grated
1 clove garlic, minced
1-1/2 tablespoons canola oil

(1) Twist and wring grated <u>thawed</u> potatoes in a cotton muslin towel, if applicable, to extract moisture from potatoes.(Not needed with regular grated potatoes).
(2) Beat eggs and egg whites in large bowl until frothy. Add potatoes. Mix in flour, salt, grated onion, and garlic.
(3) Spray pan with non-stick oil. Heat large pan over medium-high heat. Then coat with canola oil. Form spoonfuls of potato mixture into patties in pan. Cook until brown and crispy on each side. Keep warm on baking sheet in 200-degree oven.

Servings: 8
Calories: 79
Fat (g.): 4.5
Sodium: 102 mg.

JESUS RETURNS TO HEAVEN

Forty days after Jesus rose from the dead, He appeared to His disciples at Jerusalem as He had a few days earlier. Then He walked with them to Bethany and blessed them. While Jesus was blessing them, He began to rise in the air until he disappeared into a cloud. The disciples strained their eyes to get another glimpse of Him. As they did, two angels appeared and announced to them, "Why stand here looking at the sky?" Jesus will return some day in the same manner that he left.

Then Jesus led them to Bethany, and lifting his hand to heaven, he blessed them. While he was blessing them, he left them and was taken up to heaven. They worshipped him and then returned to Jerusalem filled with great joy. And they spent all of their time in the Temple, praising God. *Luke 24:50-53.*

DID YOU KNOW?

Christ, appearing to Peter after His resurrection, assured him that Jesus had not rejected him as a result of his denial. In such a loving way, Jesus does not scold his followers for their unbelief and hardness of heart, but recognized how hard it was for them to believe, and He sought to remove their difficulty by offering proofs of His resurrection.

Heavenly Asparagus Soufflé

You can rise to the occasion with this unusual dish, which works wonders with traditional entrees.

Non-stick vegetable cooking oil spray
1/4 cup whole wheat flour
1 cup skim milk
3 eggs, separated
2 cups cooked asparagus -- fresh, frozen, or canned -- mashed into small pieces
1/2 teaspoon tarragon
1/2 teaspoon marjoram
2 tablespoons fat-free Parmesan cheese, grated
1/3 cup bread crumbs

(1) Preheat oven to 350 degrees. Spray a 2-quart casserole. Place a brown paper collar around outside of casserole dish. Secure with string.
(2) In a saucepan, whisk together flour and half of the milk. When blended, add remaining milk. Stirring constantly, bring to a boil. Reduce heat and cook until thickened. Whisk in egg yolks.

Return to a boil; add asparagus, tarragon, marjoram, 1 tablespoon of grated cheese, salt and pepper. Remove from heat.

(3) Beat egg whites until stiff, then fold into asparagus mixture. Pour into casserole and sprinkle remaining cheese and bread crumbs. Bake on lowest rack for 35-40 minutes. Remove from oven and remove collar.

Note: Do not open the oven door while soufflé is baking!

Servings: 6
Calories: 105
Fat (g.): 2.5
Sodium: 498 mg.

PRAYING AND PRAISING GOD

In Philippi, Paul and Silas met a woman who had an evil spirit in her, and it mocked them. Paul cast the evil spirit out of her in the name of Jesus. The woman's owners were angry and brought them before the city judge. A riot broke out and the judges commanded that Paul and Silas be beaten and put in jail. A jailer was put in charge of them and told if he let them escape, he would be killed.

In the middle of the night Paul and Silas began praying and praising God, when a huge earthquake shook the prison. The doors of the prison opened by themselves and the chains fell off the prisoners. The jailer woke up, saw the doors open and was about to kill himself instead of being tortured and killed by the judges. Paul called out and told him everyone was still there. The jailer came to Paul and Silas, kneeled down and cried, **"Sirs, what must I do to be saved?" They replied, "Believe on the Lord Jesus and you will be saved, along with your entire household."** *Acts 16:30b-31.* And they did so.

DID YOU KNOW?
Paul and Silas were beaten and jailed in violation of their rights as Roman citizens. God is able to deliver and sustain us in even the most abusive of circumstances. When we focus on Him and all that He has done for us, our identity and inner strength will be sustained. Our inner joy and ability to praise God in difficult circumstances can result in our deliverance and our enemies admitting their need for Jesus.

Macaroni and Cheese Hallelujah

Paul and Silas prayed and praised God even when they were in prison. You'll shout for joy after you've tasted this macaroni and cheese dish.

Non-stick vegetable oil cooking spray
5 cups <u>cooked</u> macaroni, drained
1-3/4 cups lowfat cheddar cheese, shredded
1 clove garlic, minced
1 large onion, finely chopped
1/4 cup parsley, chopped
1-3/4 cups fat-free cottage cheese
1/2 cup evaporated skim milk
3 teaspoons Dijon-style mustard
1/2 teaspoon <u>each</u> salt and freshly ground pepper

(1) Preheat oven to 400 degrees.

(2) In a large bowl combine macaroni, cheddar cheese, garlic, onion, and parsley.
(3) In a blender combine cottage cheese, milk, and mustard. Process until smooth.
(4) Pour over macaroni mixture and mix thoroughly. Add salt and pepper.
(5) Spray 2-quart casserole and place mixture in it.

Topping

1 slice turkey bacon, cooked crisp
1 slice whole grain bread, crumbled
1/4 cup fat-free Parmesan cheese, grated

(1) Crumble bacon and mix with bread and cheese.
(2) Sprinkle over casserole.
(3) Bake 20-30 minutes; covered for 15-20 minutes, uncovered the remainder of the time.

Servings: 8
Calories: 238
Fat (g.): 2
Sodium: 323 mg.

JESUS' RETURN TO EARTH

And the angel showed me a pure river with the water of life, clear as crystal, flowing from the throne of God and of the Lamb, coursing down the center of the main street. On each side of the river grew a tree of life, bearing twelve crops of fruit, with a fresh crop each month. The leaves were used for medicine to heal the nations.

No longer will anything be cursed. For the throne of God and of the lamb will be there, and his servants will worship him. And they will see his face, and his name will be written on their foreheads. And there will be no night there -- no need for lamps or sun - for the Lord God will shine on them. And they will reign forever and ever.

Then the angel said to me, "These words are trustworthy and true: 'The Lord God, who tells his prophets what the future holds, has sent his angel to tell you what will happen soon.'"

"Look, I am coming soon! Blessed are those who obey the prophecy written in this scroll."

I, John, am the one who saw and heard all these things. And when I saw and heard these things, I fell down to worship the angel who showed them to me. But again he said, "No, don't worship me. I am a servant of God, just like you and your brothers the prophets, as well as all who obey what is written in this scroll. Worship God!"

Then he instructed me, "Do not seal up the prophetic words you have written, for the time is near. Let the one who is doing wrong continue to do wrong; the one who is vile, continue to be vile; the one who is good, continue to do good; and the one who is holy, continue in holiness."

"See, I am coming soon, and my reward is with me, to repay all according to their deeds. I am the Alpha and the Omega, the First and the Last, the Beginning and the End."

Blessed are those who wash their robes so they can enter through the gates of the city and eat the fruit from the tree of life. Outside the city are the dogs -- the sorcerers, the sexually immoral, the murderers, the idol worshippers, and all who love to live a lie.

"I, Jesus, have sent my angel to give you this message for the churches. I am both the source of David and the heir to his throne. I am the bright morning star."

The Spirit and the bride say, "Come." Let each one who hears them say, "Come." Let the thirsty ones come -- anyone who wants to. Let them come and drink the water of life without charge. And I solemnly declare to everyone who hears the prophetic words of this

book: If anyone adds anything to what is written here, God will add to that person plagues described in this book. And if anyone removes any of the words of this prophetic book, God will remove that person's share in the tree of life and in the holy city that are described in this book.

He who is the faithful witness to all these things says, "Yes, I am coming soon!"
Amen! Come, Lord Jesus!
The grace of the Lord Jesus be with you all. *Rev. 22:1-21.*

DID YOU KNOW?

Knowing that Christ is coming back helps us to persevere during tough times and enhances our personal relationship with Him. Having the hope of one day meeting Him face-to-face encourages us to live a life of holiness.

Strawberry Crown Cake

A crowning delight for any occasion is this magnificent 3-tiered cake, a small reminder of the crown we will someday see our King wear!

Non-stick vegetable oil cooking spray
Flour
1 pkg. yellow cake mix
1 cup water
3/4 cup egg substitute or 3 egg whites
1/3 cup applesauce
1 teaspoon vanilla

Cake:

(1) Preheat oven to 375 degrees.
(2) Place cake mix, water, egg whites, applesauce, and vanilla into mixing bowl and prepare according to package directions. Pour into <u>three</u> 8-inch pans that have been sprayed and floured. Bake according to package directions. Cool on rack for 10 minutes, and unmold onto rack. Cool completely.

Topping & Assembly:

2 <u>large</u> containers of fat-free whipped topping
2 small baskets of fresh strawberries, washed
1/2 cup almonds, slivered and toasted

(1) Hull and cut-up into small pieces <u>1</u> basket of berries; crush lightly.
(2) Place one layer of cake on footed cake plate.* Place 1-1/2 cups whipped cream, 1 to 1-1/2 cups of berries, and 2 tablespoons of almonds on the cake layer.

(3) Repeat Step 2 <u>once</u>, placing one layer on top of the other.

(3) On top layer, place a generous amount of whipped cream, sprinkle the remainder of the nuts, and place the <u>whole</u> strawberries from the second basket around the rim of the cake.

*A footed cake plate makes a better presentation, but is not required.

Servings: 8
Calories: 423
Fat (g.): 4.5
Sodium: 559 mg.

EPILOGUE

Would you like to know this Jesus Christ who is mentioned in the pages of this cookbook? He's a real person and He loves you very, very much. So much, He was willing to die for your sins. On the third day after His death, He rose from the dead. Those who put their trust in Him shall live forever with Him. Pray the following prayer (from Kenneth Copeland Ministries) out loud from your heart, and the Bible promises you will spend eternity with God.

After the first paragraph in the prayer below, God has a special present for you. It's called the Baptism in the Holy Spirit. If you'd like to receive this gift, please follow the directions in paragraphs, two, three, and four below.

Prayer for Salvation and Baptism in the Holy Spirit

Heavenly Father, I come to You in the Name of Jesus. Your Word says, ". . .whosoever shall call on the name of the Lord shall be saved" (Acts 2.21). I am calling on You. I pray and ask Jesus to come into my heart and be Lord over my life according to Romans 10:9-10. "If thou shalt confess with thy mouth the Lord Jesus, and shalt believe in thine heart that God has raised him from the dead, thou shalt be saved." I do that now. I confess that Jesus is Lord, and I believe in my heart that God raised Him from the dead.

I am now reborn! I am a Christian -- a child of Almighty God! I am saved! You also said in Your Word, "If ye then, being evil, know how to give good gifts unto your children: HOW MUCH MORE shall your heavenly Father give the Holy Spirit to them that ask him?" (Luke 11:13). I'm also asking You to fill me with the Holy Spirit. Holy Spirit, rise up within me as I praise God. I fully expect to speak with other tongues as You give me the utterance (Acts 2:4).

(Begin to praise God for filling you with the Holy Spirit. Speak those words and syllables you receive -- not in English. You have to use your own voice. God will not force you to speak.)

Now you are a Spirit-filled believer. Continue with the blessing God has given you and pray in tongues each day. You'll never be the same!

*****

If you prayed the "Prayer for Salvation" above -- welcome to the family of God! Here are a few suggestions to help you grow in your walk with Jesus Christ.

(1) Purchase a Bible, if you don't already own one. Read it every day.
(2) Talk to God everyday in your normal language. Thank and praise Him for all He has done for you. Tell Him about your hopes and struggles. Ask for His help and guidance.
(3) Ask God to lead you to a good Bible-teaching church near your home where you can grow in your faith in Christ.
(4) Tell someone you've accepted the Lord Jesus into your heart and life.

INDEX

King David's Beef Stew - pg. 58
Lamb, Bread, and Olive Oil - pg. 32
Lion's Den Chicken Cacciatore Delight - pg. 86

<u>Salads</u>
Colorful Cobb Salad - pg. 19
Garden of Eden Salad - pg. 2
Hearts of Palm Salad - pg. 117
The King Who Ate Grass Coleslaw - pg. 84
Layered Temple Salad - pg. 60
Watermelon Ark - pg. 5

<u>Sandwiches</u>
A Path Through The Red Sea Crab Rolls - pg. 26
Rebuilding The Wall Muffaletta - pg. 74
Rebuilt Temple Club Sandwich - pg. 72
Tuna Picnic Sandwich - pg. 111

<u>Side Dishes</u>
Almost There Baked Beans - pg. 42
Pentecost Pancakes - pg. 122
Good Samaritan Tabbouleh - pg. 116
Heavenly Asparagus Souffle - pg. 123
Jacob's Ladder Scalloped Potatoes - pg. 15
Macaroni and Cheese Hallelujah - pg. 125
Spicy Oven-Baked French Fries - pg. 22

<u>Soups</u>
Clam Chowder In A Boat - pg. 107
Queen Esther Vegetable Soup - pg. 76
Seafood Chowder In A Boat - pg. 107
Spicy Lentil Soup - pg. 12

<u>Vegetables</u>
Bright Eyes Carrots - pg. 100
Ten Vegetable With Pasta - pg. 30

BIBLIOGRAPHY

Crenshaw, Mary Ann, **Super Beauty,** David McKay Company, Inc., 1974.

Spiritual Renewal Bible (New Living Translation), Tyndale House Publishers, Inc., 1998.

Taylor, Kenneth N., **The Book For Children**, Tyndale House Publishers, Inc., 1970.

Unger's Bible Dictionary, Moody Press, 1957.

The Wycliffe Bible Commentary, Moody Press, 1962.